# Miniature Embroidery
## for the 20th Century Dolls' House
Projects in 1/12 Scale

# Miniature Embroidery
## for the 20th Century Dolls' House
### Projects in 1/12 Scale

Pamela Warner

GUILD OF MASTER CRAFTSMAN PUBLICATIONS LTD

First published 2003 by
Guild of Master Craftsman Publications Ltd
Castle Place, 166 High Street,
Lewes, East Sussex BN7 1XU

ISBN 1 86108 272 X

Publisher: Paul Richardson
Art Director: Ian Smith
Managing Editor: Gerrie Purcell
Commissioning Editor: April McCroskie
Editor: Olivia Underhill
Designer: Ian Hunt Design
Production Manager: Stuart Poole
Photographer: Anthony Bailey
(except for the following by Pamela Warner:
pages iv, 2–9, 17, 21, 23, 39, 43, 45, 47,
49, 51, 56, 60, 65)
Illustrator: John Yates (from sketches by Pamela Warner)

Colour origination by Universal Graphics, Singapore
Printed and bound by Stamford Press, Singapore

# Contents

For my new little granddaughter,
Francesca

# Notices

## Measurements

Although care has been taken to ensure that the metric measurements are true and accurate, they are only conversions from imperial; they have been rounded up or down to the nearest millimetre, or to the nearest convenient equivalent in cases where the imperial measurements themselves are only approximate. When following the projects, use either the metric or the imperial measurements; do not mix units. The exact size of the finished designs is dependent on the stitch count and the gauge of canvas used.

## Photocopying

Readers may find it useful to photocopy the needlepoint charts for their own private use, so that they may be enlarged; but remember that all designs in this book are copyright and may not be reproduced for any other purpose without the permission of the designer and copyright owner. Items made using the designs in this book are not to be sold without permission of the author.

## Charts

Thread colour codes refer to the threads used in the projects. The colours in the charts and the keys that accompany the charts are for reference only.

# Introduction

The projects designed for this volume are intended to give an overview of design styles during the twentieth century. However, the styles dominating at the beginning of the century were continuing developments of those in the latter part of the nineteenth century. Therefore, Chapter 2 covers designs inspired by Charles Rennie Mackintosh and Art Nouveau. Not only did the influences of the notable designers of the late nineteenth century continue well into the twentieth, but their designs were revived and remain popular today.

Although general timescales are given for the styles, they are not rigid. Needlework magazines, kits and books were produced with patterns and techniques throughout the century reflecting many styles. Even now, in the twenty-first century, cottages, flowers and Jacobean crewelwork designs are as popular as ever.

As each chapter is devoted to a style, in order to avoid constant repetition, the making up instructions for the basic items have been gathered together in Chapter 9, 'Making Up and Finishing'. General advice is given in Chapter 10, 'General Hints and Tips', under the appropriate headings and should be consulted in conjunction with the working methods for each project.

All the projects are influenced by original pieces and will give an authentic flavour to any modern dolls' house or room box.

By substituting a larger count of fabric the charts can be used to produce small-framed panels of embroidery.

# 1

# An Introduction to the styles of the 20th Century

**Fragment of a curtain showing an early move from the Arts and Crafts style to Art Nouveau. Worked in twisted silks on silk, *c.*1885**

The twentieth century heralded a time of great changes in design, style, industrial progress, transport and trade, all of which had a great influence on the way people lived and their homes. Architectural styles ranged from Edwardian, Art Deco and the suburban semi, to ultra-modern minimalism of the later twentieth century.

Much of the early part of the twentieth century continued to be heavily influenced by design trends of the late nineteenth century; the Arts and Crafts movement, William Morris' designs, Charles Rennie Mackintosh, Liberty & Co., to name just a few. Many of the leading designers continued to work until well into the twentieth century; indeed, the styles of Morris and Mackintosh enjoyed a popular revival in the late 1990s. The main characteristics of the various design styles are discussed more fully to introduce each chapter.

The Art Nouveau style spanned the turn of the nineteenth and twentieth centuries, from 1890 to World War I. The style is recognizable by its flowing sinuous lines, giving an elongated, elegant feel to the motifs.

One of the main exponents of Art Nouveau style in Britain was Charles Rennie Mackintosh who studied at the Glasgow School of Art in Scotland. Later the school had a prominent embroidery department headed by Jessie Newbery with Ann Macbeth as a tutor. Charles Rennie Mackintosh developed a very distinctive style, incorporating geometric motifs, often with the renowned Glasgow Rose.

The Art Deco style dominated the inter-war period, characterized by bold, stylized, geometric shapes, often in strong colours, reflecting the taste for all things modern.

The 1920s were famous for the beaded dresses that were the height of fashion, sometimes completely covered with heavy ornate beading, or alternatively, beaded bands that could be easily moved from garment to garment.

The shortages of materials resulting from World War II encouraged the re-use of materials. The new fabrics that were available were often of poor quality with little or no choice.

The first half of the twentieth century saw a revival of crewelwork, a style of embroidery originating from the seventeenth century and continuing into the eighteenth and nineteenth. Due to its origins, it was given the name 'Jacobean Work' in the early twentieth century. The design was based on a Tree of Life form, and worked in a variety of decorative stitches, for example long and short, stem, satin, laid fillings and French knots.

During the 1930s to 1950s there was a desire for the idyllic, possibly stemming from the austerity of the war period. Many embroidery designs featured pastoral scenes, typical English cottage gardens, and, almost always, the crinoline lady. This would be a figure

**Detail of a panel showing an Iris. Worked in silk on a black sateen ground, *c.*1900**

**Cushion cover worked in the style of Jessie Newbery, probably 1920–30**

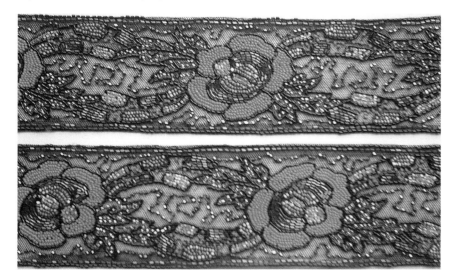

**Beaded bands for use on a dress showing a bold design of stylized roses, 1920s and 30s**

3

**Panel, typical Jacobean work in wools on a woollen twill ground, 1940s**

in a crinoline dress and bonnet, usually sideways on, to avoid having to sew a face, and often carrying a basket of flowers.

In 1934 the Needlework Development Scheme was set up in Scotland with the aim of encouraging embroidery in schools. The scheme was so successful that it was used in schools throughout the United Kingdom, and eventually was adopted by The Women's Institute and the Townswomen's Guild, who both actively encouraged crafts. Many famous designers contributed to the leaflets and books, making use of simple, bold designs and fabrics, and the style spread to North America. The aims of the scheme were thought to have been achieved by 1962, when it was disbanded.

Cross stitch has always proved to be popular and continues to be so. Usually worked from charts, it allows even the beginner to achieve a successful result. During the 1950s and 60s many designs and new materials were introduced and imported from Denmark to Britain, Europe and America. Designs varied from flowers and animals to scenes and copies of paintings.

Canvaswork, which became known as tapestry, was also popular, developed from the Berlin wool work of the nineteenth century. Many kits and coloured canvases were sold and stitched with great enthusiasm by embroiderers.

**Cheval set showing a country garden, 1940s. Stranded cotton on a cotton ground. The drawing of the trees reflects the Art Deco style**

Left **Cushion cover, showing crinoline lady in a garden, 1930–40. Stranded cotton on a linen ground**

Below **Panel with crinoline lady in appliqué on a linen ground, 1940s**

**Detail of a sampler with motifs in the style of those used in the Needlework Development Scheme, *c.*1940s**

**Cross stitch worked as a floral motif on a handkerchief sachet, 1950s**

The late 1950s brought a fashion for abstract designs with bold, modern shapes in bright colours, which continued into the following two decades. During the 1960s and 70s a revival in creative embroidery fuelled many classes and new branches of the Embroiderers' Guild. City and Guilds embroidery examination courses blossomed throughout Europe, North America and Australia and encouraged

**Hand-coloured Berlin wool work charts, 1830–40, the forerunner of those produced throughout the twentieth century**

**Detail of a cushion cover, early twentieth century**

A 'sampler' of various chain stitches, worked on a City and Guilds course in 1975

Chinese embroidered panel worked especially for export. Commissioned by Allens for their outlet in Duke Street, London in the 1970s

embroiderers to design their own original work. The strong emphasis on design brought embroidery to a high artistic level. City and Guilds and the Embroiderers' Guild continued to promote embroidery through the remaining decades of the twentieth century and have maintained that interest into the twenty-first.

The second half of the twentieth century brought wider, affordable travel, creating a great interest in foreign artefacts, food and textiles, all of which influenced fashion and interior decor. From the 1970s retail outlets were set up by specialists, who travelled with the purpose of returning with items to sell, which were used to decorate the home and the person. Items were brought from India, the Far East, the Americas, Africa, Australasia and Eastern Europe.

The following projects are designed to reflect some of the many design influences of the twentieth century, and to bring them to life within your room boxes and dolls' houses.

**Indian toran door hanging, worked in chain stitch and using shisha glass, late nineteenth to early twentieth century**

# 2

# Art Nouveau

Art Nouveau was fashionable in the cities of Europe and North America from *c.*1890 to 1910, emerging from the Arts and Crafts movement. The attractive motif designs were characterized by the use of fluid lines giving an elongated format.

Charles Rennie Mackintosh (1868–1928) was one of the main influences in Glasgow. Using organic plant forms, he combined Symbolism and Art Nouveau to add a geometric feature to his designs. A prominent motif that he used is known as the Glasgow Rose; a similar design is featured in some of the projects on the following pages.

The designers who worked in the Art Nouveau style in Europe are too numerous to mention here. However, I have based two of my projects on the work of Alphonse Mucha (1860–1939), the Czech artist who settled and worked in Paris. Famous for his posters, he is also particularly noted for his stage designs and costumes for Sarah Bernhardt. His posters featured beautiful women in flowing gowns, often against an elaborate background.

The projects in this chapter begin with a set of co-ordinating items, based on the style of Charles Rennie Mackintosh, which could be used together within a setting.

# Glasgow School Screen

This three-fold screen features a simplified version of a well-known motif of a figure and rose from a cabinet in The Mackintosh House, *c.*1900. The house was demolished in 1963, but the interior has been reconstructed at the Hunterian Art Gallery, University of Glasgow, Scotland.

## Size

Each panel: 4 x 1¼in (100 x 32mm)

Finished screen: 4¾ x 4⅛in (120 x 105mm)

## Materials

Evenweave linen, 35 count: 8 x 6in (200 x 150mm)

Stranded cotton embroidery thread as listed in key: approx. 1yd (1m) each

Tacking cotton

Small rectangular embroidery frame

Tapestry needles: No. 26 or 28

Flat stripwood, all pieces ⅛in (3mm) thick as follows:

    4 x 1½in (100 x 38mm), 3 pieces

    4 x ⅛in (100 x 3mm), 6 pieces

    1¼ x ⅛in (32 x 3mm), 6 pieces

Thin leather, felt or Vilene: 8 x 6in (200 x 150mm)

PVA wood glue

Paint or varnish as desired

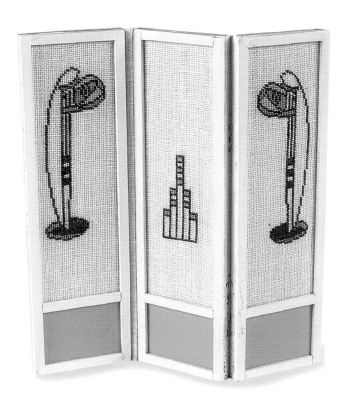

## Working method

**1** Mount the fabric into a small rectangular embroidery frame and mark the outlines of the three panels with small tacking stitches (see panel size on page 12).

**2** Mark the centre of each panel with tacking stitches. These can be removed as soon as the embroidery is started; they simply aid the placing of the first stitches.

**3** Refer to the charts, working each of the first, second and third panels. Every square on the chart represents one stitch over one thread of the fabric.

**4** Begin to stitch near to the centre to aid counting. Use one thread of stranded cotton and tent stitch throughout.

**5** When the embroidery is complete, remove from the embroidery frame.

**6** Assemble the screen using the instructions in Chapter 9, 'Making Up and Finishing'.

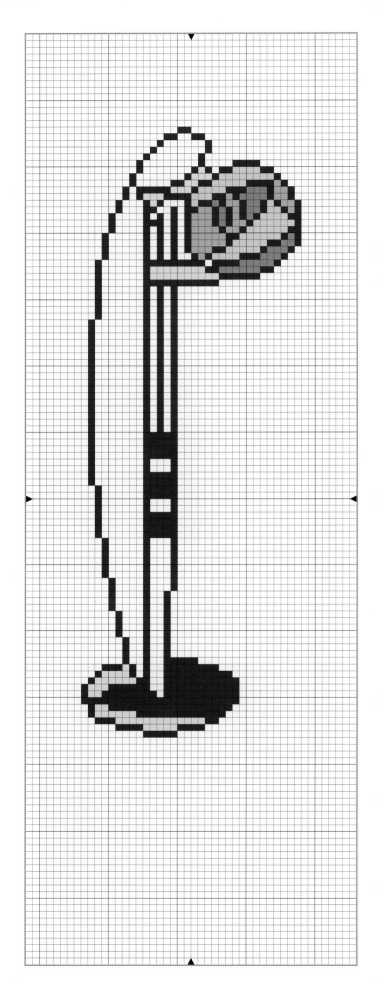

|  |  | DMC | Anchor | Madeira |
|---|---|---|---|---|
|  | Dark grey | 413 | 236 | 1713 |
|  | Green | 472 | 264 | 1414 |
|  | Purple | 550 | 102 | 0713 |
|  | Mauve | 316 | 1017 | 0809 |
|  | Lilac | 778 | 1016 | 0808 |
|  | Pink | 893 | 40 | 0413 |
|  | Background (optional) | 762 | 234 | 1804 |

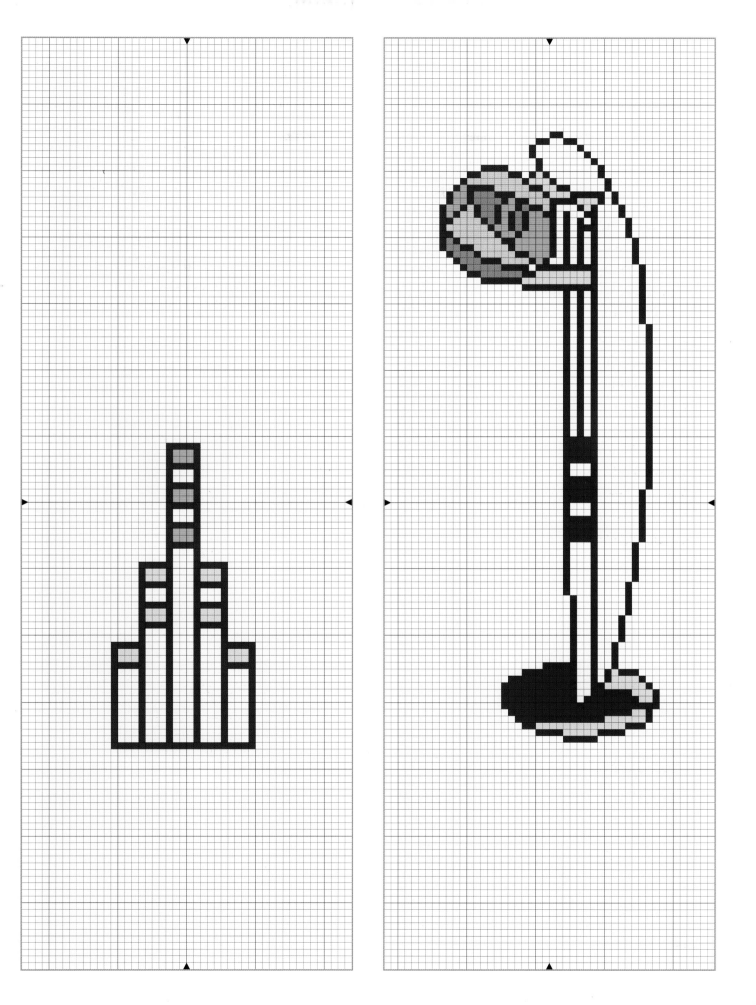

# Glasgow School Cushions

The designs for these two cushions are based on a rose motif from a leaded glass panel in a cabinet, and a leaded panel designed by Margaret Macdonald, both *c.*1900.

## Size

1¼in (32mm) square

## Materials

### For each cushion:

Evenweave linen, 32 count: 4in (100mm) square

Lightweight fabric to match for back of cushion: 4in (100mm) square

Stranded cotton embroidery thread as listed in key: approx. 1yd (1m) each

Tacking cotton

Small embroidery frame

Tapestry needles: No. 26 or 28

Sewing thread to match cushion colour

Small amount of wadding or small plastic beads for filling

|  |  | DMC | Anchor | Madeira |
|---|---|---|---|---|
|  | Dark grey | 413 | 236 | 1713 |
|  | Green | 472 | 264 | 1414 |
|  | Mauve | 316 | 1017 | 0809 |
|  | Lilac | 778 | 1016 | 0808 |
|  | Pink | 893 | 40 | 0413 |
|  | Background (optional) | 762 | 234 | 1804 |

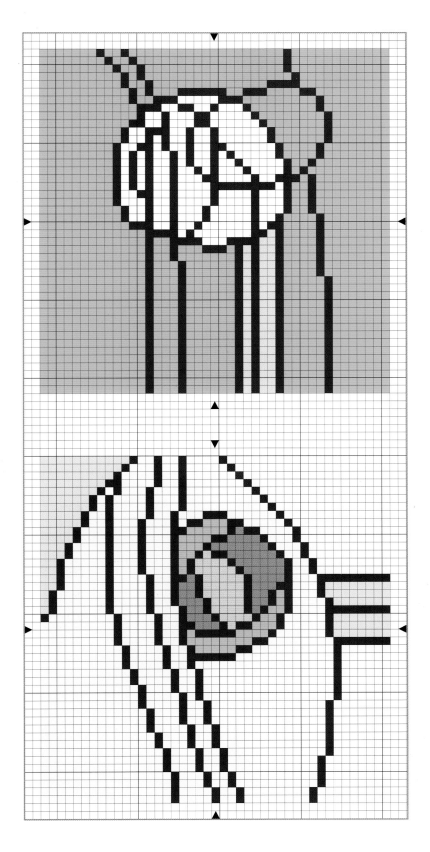

## Working method

**1** Mount the fabric into a small card mount or embroidery frame. See Chapter 10 for details.

**2** Determine the centre of the fabric and mark with a tacking stitch. This can be removed as soon as the embroidery begins.

**3** Refer to your chosen chart and begin to stitch from the centre. Each square on the chart represents one stitch over one thread of the fabric. Use one thread of stranded cotton and tent stitch throughout.

**4** When the embroidery is complete, remove the fabric from the frame.

**5** Make up the cushion as described in Chapter 9.

# Glasgow School Carpet

The design for this little carpet was inspired by an example designed for a bedroom in Hill House, *c*.1902. The simplicity perfectly reflects the clean lines of Mackintosh's interior.

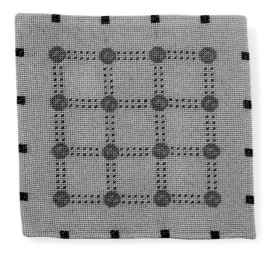

## Size

5in (126mm) square

## Materials

Mono canvas or coin net, 24 count: 7in (180mm) square

Stranded embroidery thread as listed in key: approx. 2yd (2m) each, 3 skeins background colour

Tacking cotton

Small rectangular embroidery frame

Tapestry needles: No. 24

## Working method

**1** Mount the canvas in a small rectangular embroidery frame; do not use a round frame as it will distort the canvas.

**2** Using tacking thread, mark the vertical and horizontal centre lines with stitches.

**3** Important: do not work the third row in from the edges as this row is worked last in order to form a flat hem. See the instructions in Chapter 9.

**4** Referring to the chart, begin to stitch in the centre until enough of the design has been worked to give a reference. Each square on the chart represents one stitch over one thread of the canvas. Use two strands of stranded cotton and tent stitch throughout.

**5** When the embroidery is complete, remove from the frame. Sometimes the canvas will distort even when a frame is used. If this happens you may need to block the carpet back into shape. Instructions appear in Chapter 10.

**6** On completion, and after blocking, complete the hem by working the third row in from the edge as shown in Chapter 9.

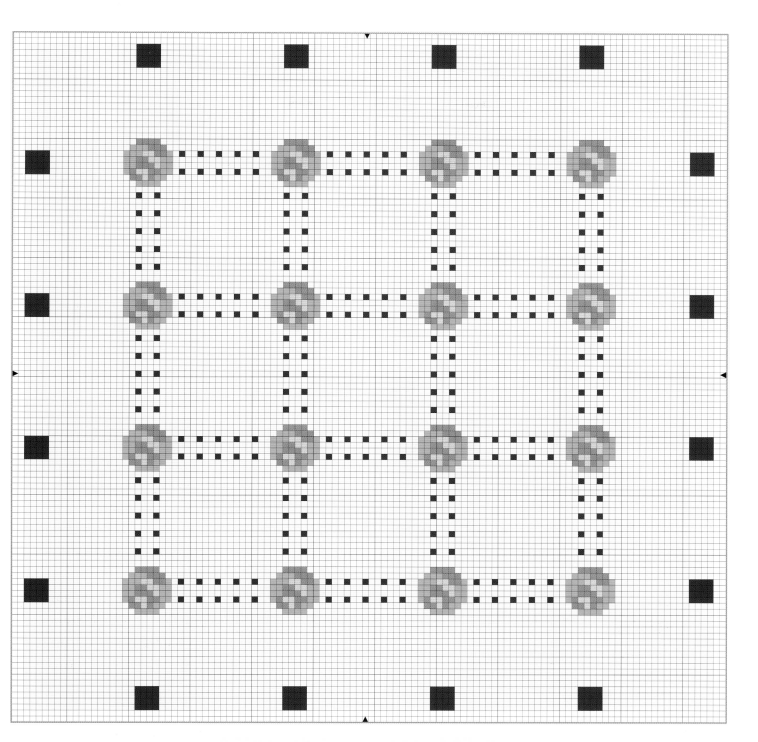

| | | DMC | Anchor | Madeira |
|---|---|---|---|---|
| ⬛ | Dark grey | 413 | 236 | 1713 |
| ▨ | Mauve | 316 | 1017 | 0809 |
| ▨ | Lilac | 778 | 1016 | 0808 |
| ▨ | Pink | 893 | 40 | 0413 |
| ⬜ | Background | Ecru | 926 | Ecru |

# Glasgow School Bedcover

A rose motif features again in the design for this bedcover. Although shown as a double bed size, a single size can be achieved by reducing the number of threads between the motifs.

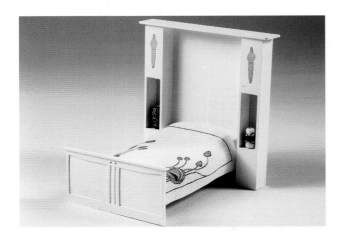

## Size

6in (150mm) square, or as desired

## Materials

Evenweave linen, 35 count: 8in (200mm) square

Stranded cotton embroidery thread as listed in key: approx. 1yd (1m) each

Tacking cotton

Small rectangular embroidery frame

Tapestry needles: No. 26 or 28

## Working method

**1**  Mount the fabric into a small rectangular embroidery frame.

**2**  Using tacking thread, mark the vertical and horizontal centres of the fabric, and use these lines to measure and mark the outside edges of the bedcover to the required size.

**3**  Referring to the chart, you will see that each square on the chart represents one stitch over one thread of the fabric. Use one thread of stranded cotton and tent stitch throughout.

**4**  As there are not any embroidery stitches near the centre, is it easier to begin this project at one of the lower corners. Leave 18 threads of the linen as a border. Reverse the chart to work the mirror image.

**5**  When the embroidery is complete, remove from frame, and make up as shown in Chapter 9.

|  |  | DMC | Anchor | Madeira |
|---|---|---|---|---|
|  | Dark grey | 413 | 236 | 1713 |
|  | Green | 472 | 264 | 1414 |
|  | Purple | 550 | 102 | 0713 |
|  | Mauve | 316 | 1017 | 0809 |
|  | Lilac | 778 | 1016 | 0808 |
|  | Pink | 893 | 40 | 0413 |

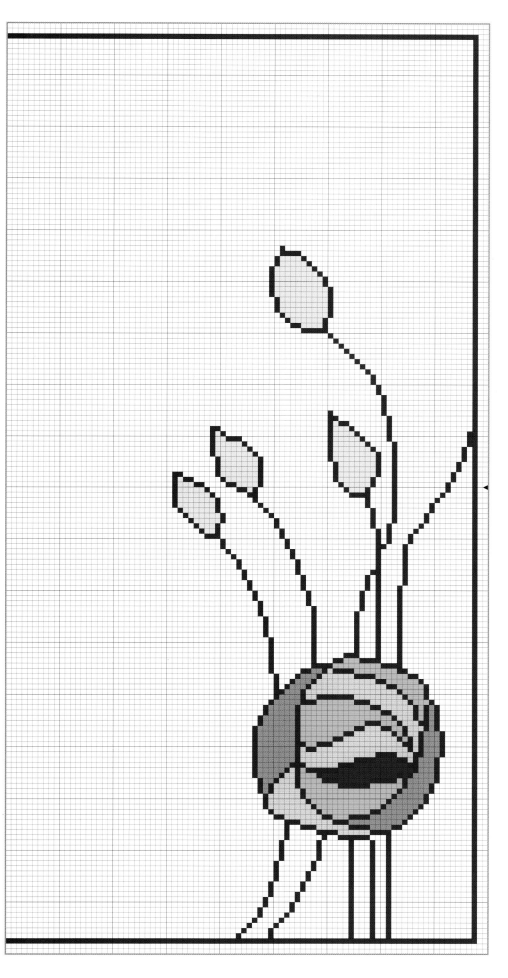

# Wall Hangings in the style of Alphonse Mucha

These two designs for wall hangings are inspired by poster designs by Alphonse Mucha representing Topaz and Ruby. The flowing lines and highly decorative background patterns are typical of his style. The hangings can be mounted within mouldings, as shown, or made up as free-hanging panels. Full instructions are given in Chapter 9.

## Size

Each panel, 35 count: 5 x 2⅛in (127 x 54mm)

## Materials

### For both panels:

Evenweave linen, 35 count: 9 x 8in (230 x 200mm)

Stranded cotton embroidery thread as listed in key: approx. 1yd (1m) each

Tacking cotton

Rectangular embroidery frame

Tapestry needles: No. 26 or 28

Miniature picture frame moulding if desired

| | | DMC | Anchor | Madeira |
|---|---|---|---|---|
| | Dark green | 501 | 877 | 1704 |
| | Mid green | 3053 | 260 | 1603 |
| | Light green | 504 | 1042 | 1701 |
| | Dark brown | 839 | 1050 | 1913 |
| | Rust | 920 | 1004 | 0312 |
| | Dark grey | 413 | 236 | 1713 |
| | Red | 815 | 43 | 0512 |
| | Light red | 606 | 334 | 0209 |
| | Orange | 970 | 316 | 0204 |
| | Peach | 945 | 881 | 2313 |
| | Cream | 677 | 886 | 2207 |
| | Dark flesh | 950 | 376 | 2309 |
| | Light flesh | 951 | 880 | 2308 |
| | Light grey | 415 | 398 | 1802 |
| | Shaded gold or metallic | 90 or metallic | 1219 or metallic | metallic |

By selecting the top sections of each charted design, a framed picture can be worked.

## Working method

**1** Mount the fabric into a rectangular embroidery frame and, using tacking cotton, mark the outer edges of the hanging with tacking stitches.

**2** Refer to the charts on pages 24–27. Each square represents one stitch over one thread of the canvas. Use one strand of stranded cotton and tent stitch throughout.

**3** Begin to stitch at one of the top corners. Once a section of stitching has been worked, it is easy to progress down the design.

**4** Do not leave a gap between the two halves of the chart.

**5** When the embroidery is complete, remove from the frame and make up or mount as desired. Instructions for both methods are in Chapter 9.

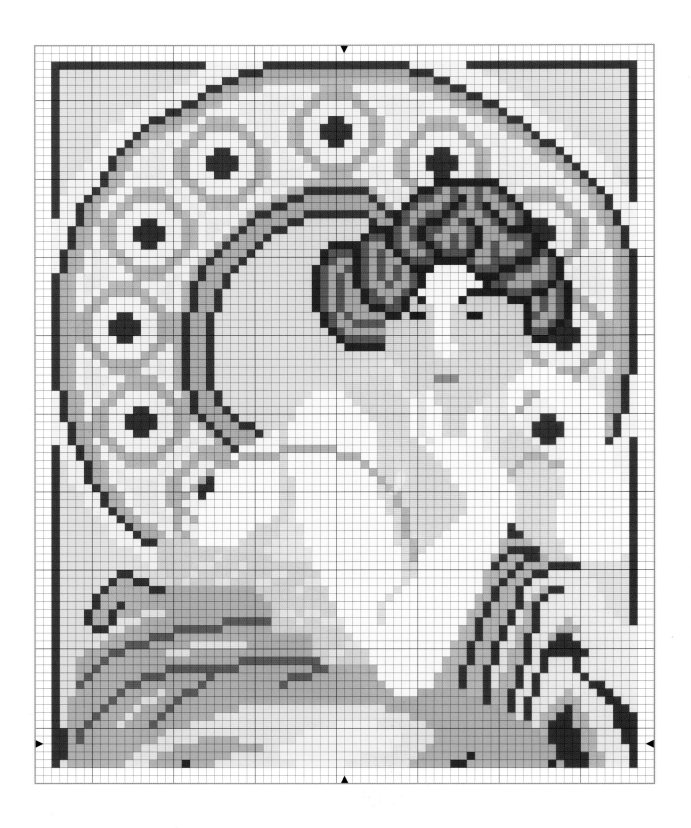

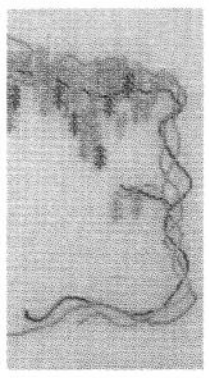

# Wisteria Screen and Wall Hanging

The delicate intertwining stems and hanging blossoms that form this design are very typical of the Art Nouveau style. The design passes across the three panels of the screen to form a whole. By working the design with all three panels joined together, a wall hanging can be achieved, which can be either mounted within panelling or made up as a free-hanging panel.

## Size

Area of embroidery, 35 count: 4¾ x 1⅜in (120 x 35mm)

## Materials

Evenweave linen, 35 count: 8 x 6in (200 x 150mm)

Stranded cotton embroidery thread as listed in key: approx. 1yd (1m) each

Tacking cotton

Rectangular embroidery frame

Tapestry needles: No. 26 or 28

Flat stripwood, all pieces ⅛in (3mm) thick, as follows:

   5⅛ x 1⅝in (130 x 40mm), 3 pieces

   5⅛ x ⅛in (130 x 3mm), 6 pieces

   1⅜ x ⅛in (35 x 3mm), 3 pieces

   1⅜ x ¼in (35 x 6mm), 3 pieces

Thin leather, Vilene or felt: 8 x 6in (200 x 150mm)

PVA wood glue

Paint or varnish as desired

# Screen

## Working method

**1** Mount the fabric into a small rectangular embroidery frame and mark the outlines of the three panels side by side with about 1in (25mm) between each.

**2** Mark the centre of each panel with a tacking stitch, which will be removed as soon as the embroidery is under way.

**3** Refer to the charts on pages 30–31, begin with the stems of the design. Each square on the chart represents one stitch over one thread of the fabric. Use one strand of stranded cotton and tent stitch throughout.

**4** As there are open areas of fabric which are not worked, try not to take threads across the back of the fabric behind these areas, as the thread may show through when the item is mounted.

**5** When the embroidery is complete, remove from the frame. Mount the embroidery and assemble the screen as directed in Chapter 9.

| | | DMC | Anchor | Madeira |
|---|---|---|---|---|
| | Light grey | 928 | 274 | 1708 |
| | Mid grey | 453 | 231 | 1806 |
| | Dark grey | 451 | 233 | 1808 |
| | Light mauve | 211 | 342 | 0801 |
| | Mauve | 554 | 96 | 0711 |
| | Pink | 778 | 1016 | 0808 |
| | Light green | 504 | 1042 | 1701 |
| | Dark green | 502 | 876 | 1703 |

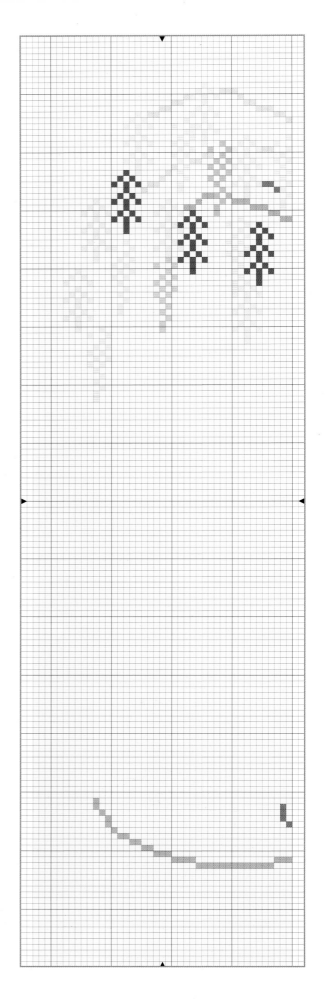

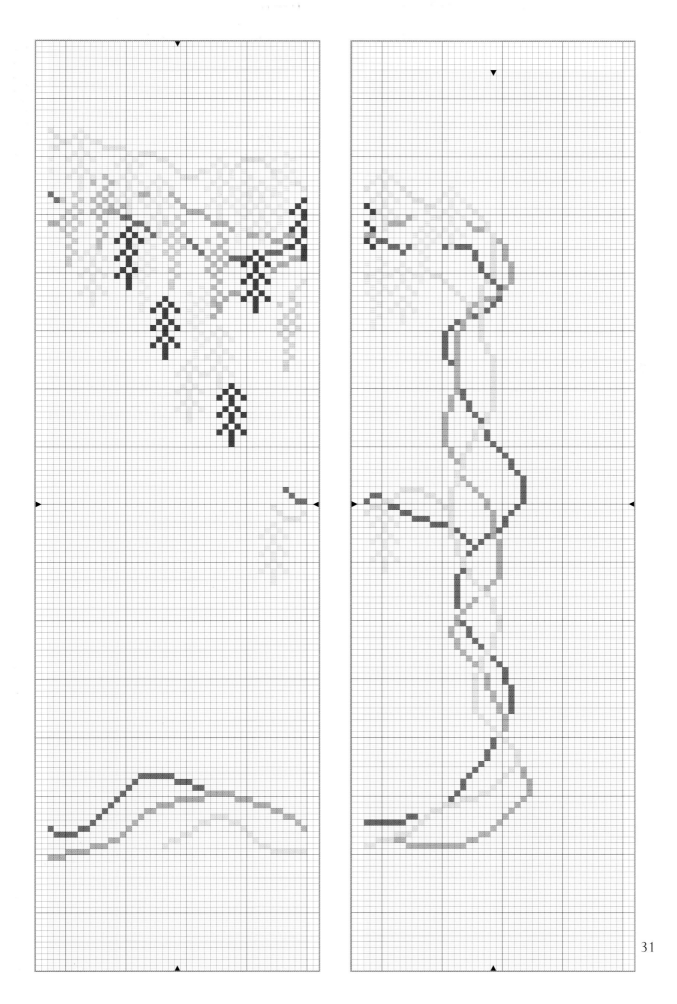

# Wall Hanging

This charming wall hanging is a perfect complement to the Wisteria Screen (see pages 29–31). The pinks, mauves and greens used in both items are typical of the Art Nouveau era.

## Size

On 35 count: 4¾ x 4in (120 x 100mm)

On 40 count: 4⅜ x 3¾in (110 x 95mm)

## Materials

Evenweave linen, 35 count: 8 x 6in (200 x 150mm)

Stranded cotton embroidery thread as listed in key: approx. 1yd (1m) each

Tacking cotton

Rectangular embroidery frame

Tapestry needles: No. 26 or 28

## Working method

**1**  Mount the fabric in a small rectangular embroidery frame, marking the outlines of the panel.

**2**  Mark the centre of the panel with a tacking stitch, which will be removed as soon as the embroidery is under way.

**3**  Refer to the charts, as for Wisteria Screen (pages 30–31), and begin with the stems of the design. Each square on the chart represents one stitch over one thread of the fabric. Use one strand of stranded cotton and tent stitch throughout.

**4**  Do not leave any space between the sections, as was instructed for the screen (see pages 28–31).

**5**  As there are open areas of fabric which are not worked, try not to take threads across the back of the fabric behind these areas as the thread may show through when the item is mounted.

**6**  When the embroidery is complete, remove from the frame.

**7**  Make up the wall hanging using one of the methods described in Chapter 9.

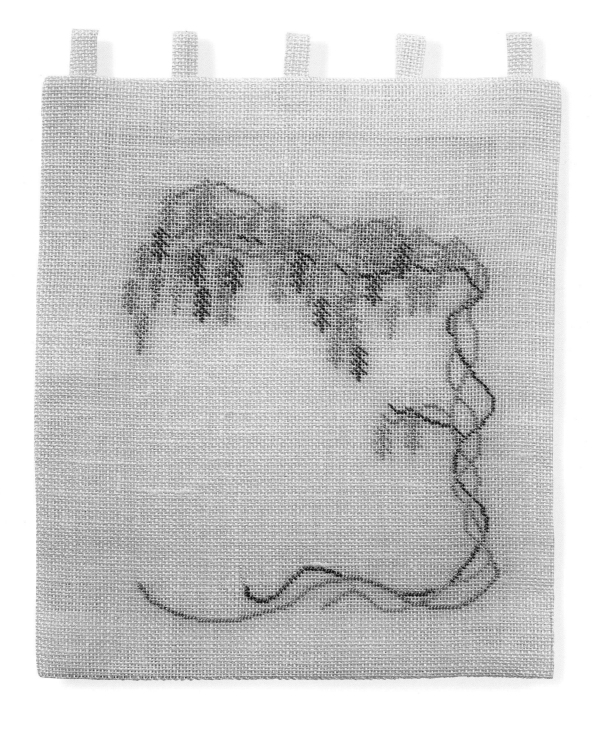

# 3

# Art Deco

Art Deco is the name given to the 'Moderne' style that dominated the 1920s and 30s. The style was greatly influenced by the teaching at the Bauhaus school of architectural design in Germany, and by the Cubism movement in art.

The use of bold, geometric shapes and shiny surfaces makes it easily recognizable, differing greatly from the fluid lines of Art Nouveau. The style was widely used in architecture, furnishings and textiles. On of the most popular motifs used in Art Deco designs was the stylized leaping gazelle.

In the field of decorative ceramic design, probably the best-known name is Clarice Cliff, (1899–1972). Her use of simplified plant and landscape motifs in bright yellow, orange, mauve and green can be seen on many examples in books and museum collections.

As with Art Nouveau, Art Deco is enjoying a revival in the twenty-first century, with museums such as the Victoria and Albert featuring dedicated displays and exhibitions.

# Leaping Gazelle Carpet

This little carpet shows the leaping gazelle motif within geometric shapes and is typical of the design of carpets and rugs of the 1920s and 30s.

The size of the carpet can be increased, if desired, by using a larger count of canvas, and increasing the number of sewing threads used.

## Working method

**1** Mount the fabric into a small rectangular embroidery frame and mark the vertical and horizontal centres.

**2** Refer to the chart, and begin working in the centre. Each square on the chart represents one stitch over one thread of canvas. Use two strands of stranded cotton and tent stitch throughout.

**3** Remember, do not work the third row in from the edge as this is used to complete the hem of the carpet (see Chapter 9).

**4** Complete the design first, then fill in the background; this will neaten the stitching on the back.

**5** When complete, remove from the frame. The carpet may need blocking back into shape if it has distorted; this must be done before the edges are turned. Instructions for this are in Chapter 10.

**6** Make up as directed in Chapter 9.

### Size

5 x 3in (126 x 75mm)

### Materials

Single-thread canvas, 24 count: 8 x 5in (200 x 126mm)

Stranded cotton embroidery thread as listed in key: approx. 1yd (1m) each. 1 skein for background colour

Small rectangular embroidery frame

Tapestry needles: No. 26 or 28

|  |  | DMC | Anchor | Madeira |
|---|---|---|---|---|
|  | Dark brown | 898 | 360 | 2006 |
|  | Mid brown | 435 | 1046 | 2010 |
|  | Orange | 740 | 316 | 0202 |
|  | Light brown (background) | 437 | 362 | 2012 |

# Leaping Gazelle Cushion

The carpet design has been adapted to a square, and is shown here as a cushion. The chart could be used for any square item, such as a fire screen or picture.

## Working method

**1** Mount the fabric into a small embroidery frame or card mount as described in Chapter 10.

**2** Using tacking cotton, mark the vertical and horizontal centres of the evenweave fabric. These can be removed once a few stitches have been worked.

**3** Refer to the chart, and begin working in the centre. Each square on the chart represents one stitch over one thread of the linen. Use one strand of stranded cotton and tent stitch throughout.

**4** When complete remove from the frame.

**5** Make up the cushion as directed in Chapter 9.

## Size

1¼in (32mm) square

## Materials

Evenweave linen, 35 count: 4in (100mm) square

Lightweight fabric for back of cushion: 4in (100mm) square

Stranded cotton embroidery thread as listed in key: approx. 1yd (1m) each. ½ skein for background

Tacking cotton

Small rectangular embroidery frame or card mount

Tapestry needles: No. 26 or 28

Sewing thread to match cushion colour

Small amount of wadding or small plastic beads for filling

| | | DMC | Anchor | Madeira |
|---|---|---|---|---|
| ■ | Dark brown | 898 | 360 | 2006 |
| ■ | Mid brown | 435 | 1046 | 2010 |
| ■ | Orange | 740 | 316 | 0202 |
| ■ | Light brown (background) | 437 | 362 | 2012 |

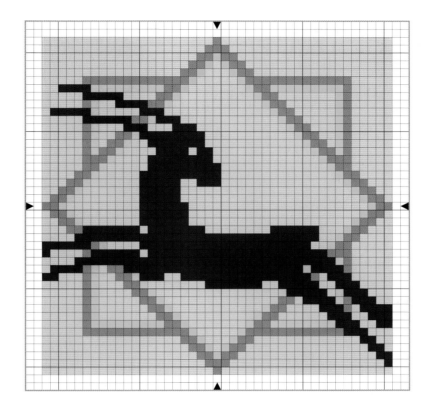

# The Eltham Palace Carpet

This project was inspired by a visit to Eltham Palace in south London, the former home of the Courtauld family, which has been magnificently restored to show an Art Deco interior. In the circular entrance hall is a carpet, which is a copy of the original, made by Marion Dorn. The original, 19ft (5.8m) in diameter, is now in the Victoria and Albert Museum in London.

The design shows the typical geometric shapes of the period.

## Working method

**1**   Mount the fabric into a small embroidery frame and mark the vertical and horizontal centres with tacking cotton.

**2**   Refer to the chart, and begin working from the centre. Each square on the chart represents one stitch over one thread of the canvas. Use one strand of stranded cotton and tent stitch throughout.

**3**   For circular carpets the finishing of the edges is different and you can work the whole carpet.

**4**   When the embroidery is complete remove from the frame. If the piece has distorted, you may need to block the carpet. This must be done before the edges are turned. Instructions for this are given in Chapter 10.

**5**   Complete the edges as instructed in Chapter 9.

### Size

5⅛in (130mm) diameter

### Materials

Single-thread canvas, 24 count: 8in (200mm) square

Stranded cotton embroidery thread as listed in key: approx. ½ skein each

Tacking cotton

Small rectangular embroidery frame

Tapestry needles: No. 26 or 28

|  |  | DMC | Anchor | Madeira |
|---|---|---|---|---|
|  | Dark red | 902 | 897 | 0601 |
|  | Medium red | 221 | 1015 | 0811 |
|  | Clover pink | 223 | 895 | 0812 |
|  | Light clover | 224 | 893 | 0813 |
|  | Light grey | 453 | 231 | 1806 |

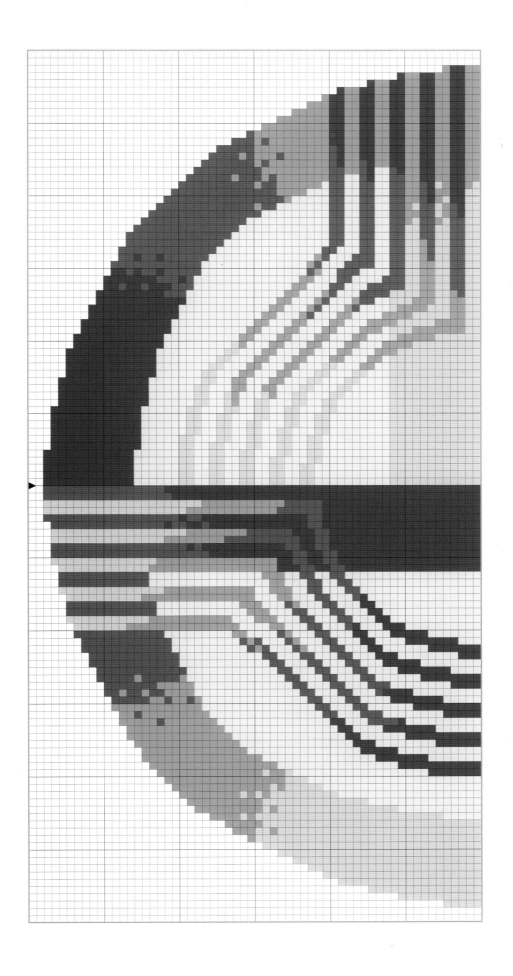

# The Eltham Palace Cushion

Here is a little cushion to complement the Eltham Palace carpet. The square format can be used for other items such as fire screens and pictures, or used as a repeat motif for larger items.

## Working method

**1** Mount the fabric into a small embroidery frame or card mount and mark the vertical and horizontal centres with tacking stitches. These tacking stitches can be removed once a few embroidery stitches have been worked.

**2** Refer to the chart, and begin to work from the centre. Each square on the chart represents one stitch over one thread of the linen. Use one strand of stranded cotton and tent stitch throughout.

**3** When the embroidery is complete remove from the frame.

**4** Make up the cushion as instructed in Chapter 9.

---

### Size

1¼in (32mm) square

### Materials

Evenweave linen, 35 count: 4in (100mm) square

Lightweight fabric to match for back of cushion: 4in (100mm) square

Stranded cotton embroidery thread as listed in key: approx. 1yd (1m) each

Tacking cotton

Small rectangular embroidery frame or card mount

Sewing thread to match cushion

Small amount of wadding or small plastic beads for filling

| | | DMC | Anchor | Madeira |
|---|---|---|---|---|
| | Dark red | 902 | 897 | 0601 |
| | Medium red | 221 | 1015 | 0811 |
| | Clover pink | 223 | 895 | 0812 |
| | Light clover | 224 | 893 | 0813 |

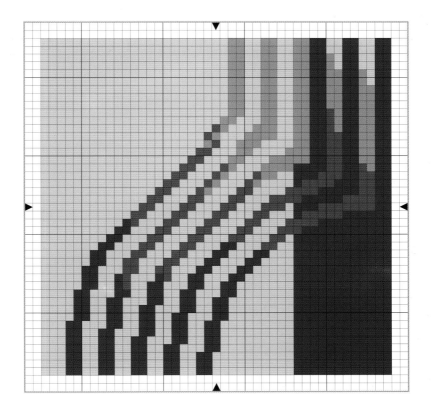

# Clarice Cliff Cushions

The next three projects are based on the stylized designs found on the popular ceramics designed by Clarice Cliff. They show the typical colours used in the originals: orange, yellow, green, blue and mauve, with details picked out in black.

## The Tree

### Size

1¼in (32mm) square

### Materials

Evenweave linen, 35 count: 4in (100mm) square

Lightweight fabric for back of cushion: 4in (100mm) square

Stranded cotton embroidery thread as listed in key: approx. 1yd (1m) each

Tacking cotton

Small rectangular embroidery frame

Sewing thread to match cushion

Small amount of wadding or small plastic beads for filling

### Working method

**1**   Mount the fabric into a small embroidery frame or card mount and mark the vertical and horizontal centres with tacking stitches. These tacking stitches can be removed once a few embroidery stitches have been worked.

**2**   Refer to the chart, and begin to work from the centre. Each square on the chart represents one stitch over one thread of the linen. Use one strand of stranded cotton and tent stitch throughout.

**3**   When complete remove from the frame.

**4**   Make up the cushion as directed in Chapter 9.

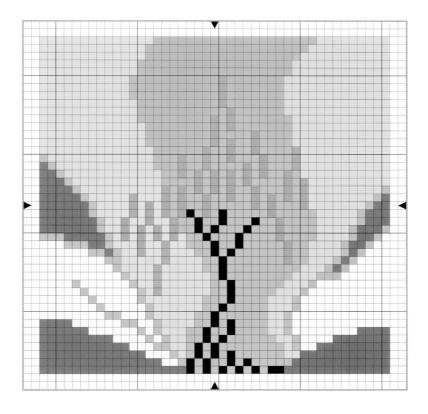

| | | DMC | Anchor | Madeira |
|---|---|---|---|---|
| | Orange | 741 | 314 | 0201 |
| | Yellow | 743 | 305 | 0113 |
| | Ecru | Ecru | 926 | Ecru |
| | Green | 470 | 266 | 1410 |
| | Blue | 799 | 145 | 0910 |
| | Black | 310 | Black | Black |

# The Crocus

## Size

1¼in (32mm)

## Materials

Evenweave linen, 35 count: 4in (100mm) square

Lightweight fabric for back of cushion: 4in (100mm) square

Stranded cotton embroidery thread as listed in key: approx. 1yd (1m) each

Tacking cotton

Small rectangular embroidery frame

Sewing thread to match cushion

Small amount of wadding or small plastic beads for filling

## Working method

**1**  Mount the fabric into a small embroidery frame or card mount and mark the vertical and horizontal centres with tacking stitches. These tacking stitches can be removed once a few embroidery stitches have been worked.

**2**  Refer to the chart, and begin to work from the centre. Each square on the chart represents one stitch over one thread of the linen. Use one strand of stranded cotton and tent stitch throughout.

**3**  When complete remove from the frame.

**4**  Make up the cushion as directed in Chapter 9.

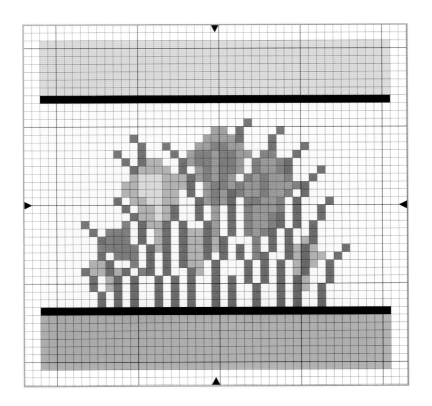

|  | | DMC | Anchor | Madeira |
|---|---|---|---|---|
|  | Orange | 741 | 314 | 0201 |
|  | Yellow | 743 | 305 | 0113 |
|  | Ecru | Ecru | 926 | Ecru |
|  | Green | 470 | 266 | 1410 |
|  | Blue | 799 | 145 | 0910 |
|  | Black | 310 | Black | Black |
|  | Mauve | 553 | 99 | 0711 |

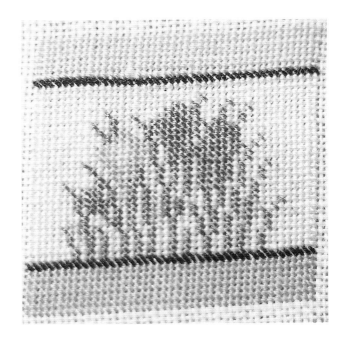

# The Cottage

## Size

1¼in (32mm) square

## Materials

Evenweave linen, 35 count: 4in (100mm) square

Lightweight fabric for back of cushion: 4in (100mm) square

Stranded cotton embroidery thread as listed in key: approx. 1yd (1m) each

Tacking cotton

Small rectangular embroidery frame

Sewing thread to match cushion

Small amount of wadding or small plastic beads for filling

## Working method

**1** Mount the fabric into a small embroidery frame or card mount and mark the vertical and horizontal centres with tacking stitches. These tacking stitches can be removed once a few embroidery stitches have been worked.

**2** Refer to the chart, and begin to work from the centre. Each square on the chart represents one stitch over one thread of the linen. Use one strand of stranded cotton and tent stitch throughout.

**3** When complete remove from the frame.

**4** Make up the cushion as directed in Chapter 9.

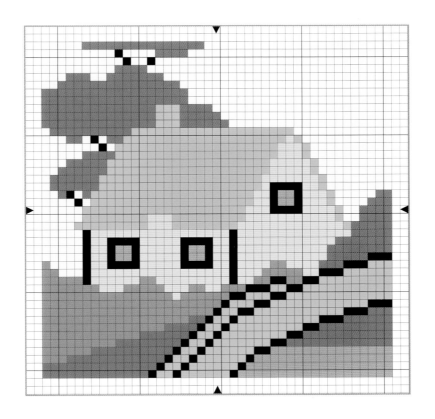

| | | DMC | Anchor | Madeira |
|---|---|---|---|---|
| | Orange | 741 | 314 | 0201 |
| | Yellow | 743 | 305 | 0113 |
| | Ecru | Ecru | 926 | Ecru |
| | Green | 470 | 266 | 1410 |
| | Blue | 799 | 145 | 0910 |
| | Black | 310 | Black | Black |
| | Mauve | 553 | 99 | 0711 |

# Green Bedcover

The design for this bedcover is based on the Dining Room doors at Eltham Palace in south London. It is a version of the ancient Greek key design which was a popular motif in the Art Deco era. The chart could be adapted for a carpet or for panels in a screen.

The linen has been dyed green before being embroidered. Coloured linens are available, but in a limited range. By dying your own you can obtain the exact colour you require. If you use fabric dyes and follow the manufacturer's instructions for setting the colour, and then the item can be washed if desired. However, any colouring medium can be used if the item is not to be washed. As linen has a natural oil within the fibres, more than one application of dye may be required to obtain a deeper colour.

## Working method

**1** Colour the fabric if desired. Further hints for this can be found in Chapter 10.

**2** Mount the fabric into a small embroidery frame and mark the vertical and horizontal centres with tacking stitches.

**3** Place a second row of tacking stitches 1in (25mm) above the horizontal centre. This gives the position of the centre of the embroidery design allowing for the bedcover to fall at the foot of the bed. If your bedcover is only covering the top of the bed, ignore Step 4.

**4** Begin to work the design from the new centre mark. Each square on the chart represents one stitch over two threads of the linen. Using one strand of stranded cotton, cross stitch over two threads throughout.

**5** When the embroidery is complete remove from the frame.

**6** Make up as directed in Chapter 9.

---

### Size

Embroidered area: 3 x 2⅝in (75 x 65mm)

Bedcover: 6in (150mm), or to the desired size

### Materials

Evenweave linen, 35 count: 8in (200mm) square, or 2in (50mm) larger than desired finished size

Lightweight Habutai silk or cotton lawn for lining: size as for evenweave linen (see above)

Stranded cotton embroidery thread as listed in key: approx. 1yd (1m) each

Tacking cotton

Small rectangular embroidery frame

Sewing thread to match fabric colour

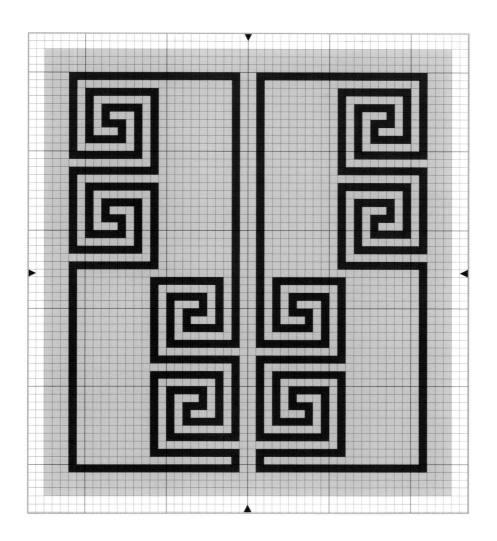

| | DMC | Anchor | Madeira |
|---|---|---|---|
| Dark green or choice | 500 | 879 | 1705 |

# 4

# The Jacobean Revival

During the 1930s and 40s there was a fashion for designs reflecting the crewelwork of the seventeenth century.

The design of early examples was based on the ancient motif of the Tree of Life, a plant form growing from a mound of earth. During the seventeenth century this was depicted in an exaggerated form with exotic foliage, birds and beasts. The Rococo period of the eighteenth century brought a lighter, more open form.

With the twentieth century came the name 'Jacobean'. The revival of these designs appeared in the many needlework magazines available. Most of the domestic embroidery was worked on household items such as cushions, fire screens and table linen, with the modern variations of the earlier designs dominating.

The early examples were mostly worked in worsted wools, hence the name crewelwork. The twentieth-century items were usually in stranded cottons when used on household items that required washing, but screens and fire screens can be found worked in wools.

# Three-fold Screen

This project reflects the typical style of crewelwork in the 1930s, 40s and even into the 50s. The plant form is elaborated with large exotic leaves growing from a mound.

## Size

Each embroidered panel: 1⅛ x 2⅜in (28 x 60mm)

Each screen panel: 1⅜ x 4½in (35 x 115mm)

Finished screen size: 4⅛ x 4½in (105 x 115mm)

## Materials

Evenweave linen, 40 count: 10 x 8in (250 x 200mm)

Stranded cotton embroidery thread as listed in key: approx. 1yd (1m) each

Tacking cotton

Small rectangular embroidery frame

Tapestry needles: No. 26 or 28

Flat stripwood: all pieces ⅛in (3mm) thick, as follows:

    1⅜ x 4½in (35 x 115mm), 3 pieces

    4½ x ⅛in (115 x 3mm), 6 pieces

    1⅜ x ⅛in (35 x 3mm), 6 pieces (to be trimmed)

Thin leather, felt or Vilene: 8 x 6in (200 x 150mm)

PVA wood glue

Paint or varnish as desired

| | | DMC | Anchor | Madeira |
|---|---|---|---|---|
| | Dark green | 319 | 683 | 1313 |
| | Medium green | 320 | 216 | 1311 |
| | Light green | 3348 | 254 | 1604 |
| | Dark brown | 839 | 1050 | 1913 |
| | Light brown | 841 | 378 | 1911 |
| | Dark blue | 517 | 169 | 1107 |
| | Medium blue | 996 | 433 | 1103 |
| | Light blue | 807 | 168 | 1109 |
| | Dark pink | 892 | 28 | 0412 |
| | Medium pink | 352 | 9 | 0303 |
| | Light pink | 776 | 24 | 0607 |
| | Dark mauve | 553 | 99 | 0711 |
| | Medium mauve | 554 | 96 | 0711 |
| | Light mauve | 778 | 1016 | 0808 |
| | Yellow | 725 | 305 | 0106 |

## Working method

**1** Mount the fabric into a small rectangular embroidery frame and mark the outlines of the three panels with small tacking stitches. Leave at least 1in (25mm) in between the panels (see page 54 for sizes).

**2** Mark the vertical and horizontal centres of each panel with tacking stitches.

**3** Refer to the chart, on page 55 and begin working near the centre of each panel. Each square on the chart represents one stitch over one thread of the linen. Use one strand of stranded cotton and tent stitch throughout.

**4** When the embroidery is complete remove from the frame.

**5** Assemble the screen and mount the panels as directed in Chapter 9.

# Wall Hanging

This project uses the same design and chart as the three-fold screen (see pages 54–56). The increase in size is due to the use of a larger-count fabric.

## Working method

**1** Mount the fabric into a small embroidery frame and mark the vertical and horizontal centres with tacking stitches.

**2** Refer to the chart, and begin to stitch in the centre. Each square on the chart represents one stitch over one thread of the fabric. Use one strand of stranded cotton, and cross stitch throughout.

**3** When the embroidery is complete, remove from the frame.

**4** Make up the wall hanging as directed in Chapter 9.

---

### Size

2⅛ x 4½in (54 x 115mm)

### Materials

Aida fabric, 18 count: 5 x 7in (126 x 180mm)

Stranded cotton embroidery thread as listed in key for Three-fold Screen (see page 54): approx. 1yd (1m) each

Tacking cotton

Small rectangular embroidery frame

Tapestry needles: No. 26 or 28

# Two Jacobean Cushion Designs

This design theme was very popular for household items, but particularly cushions.

Here are two designs, the first based on the Tree of Life, and the second on a bowl of flowers.

**Size**

1¼in (32mm) square

Selecting a 35 count will give a larger cushion

**Materials**

Evenweave linen, 40 count: 4in (100mm) square

Lightweight fabric for the back of the cushion: 4in (100mm) square

Stranded cotton embroidery thread as listed in key: approx. 1yd (1m) each

Tacking cotton

Small rectangular embroidery frame or card mount

Tapestry needles: No. 26 or 28

Sewing thread to match the cushion

Small amount of wadding or small plastic beads for filling

# Cushion 1

The design for this project was inspired by a copy of *Needlewoman and Needlecraft* (No. 33, January 1948). The design was called Chatsworth and included a transfer priced 10½ old pence, about 5p.

| | | DMC | Anchor | Madeira |
|---|---|---|---|---|
| | Dark brown | 610 | 889 | 2106 |
| | Light brown | 612 | 888 | 2108 |
| | Dark blue | 820 | 134 | 0904 |
| | Light blue | 798 | 137 | 0911 |
| | Purple | 550 | 102 | 0713 |
| | Mauve | 554 | 858 | 1511 |
| | Orange | 740 | 316 | 0202 |
| | Yellow | 725 | 305 | 0106 |
| | Dark green | 500 | 879 | 1705 |
| | Medium green | 904 | 258 | 1413 |
| | Light green | 907 | 255 | 1410 |

## Working method

**1**  Mount the fabric into a small embroidery frame or card mount and mark the vertical and horizontal centres with tacking cotton.

**2**  Refer to the chart, and begin working from the centre. Each square on the chart represents one stitch over one thread of the linen. Use one strand of stranded cotton and tent stitch throughout.

**3**  When the embroidery is complete remove from the frame.

**4**  Make up the cushion as directed in Chapter 9.

# Fire Screen

This project uses the same chart and colours as cushion design No. 1 (see pages 58–59).

## Working method

**1** Follow Steps 1 and 2 for Cushion 1, for mounting and marking up.

**2** When stitching, follow Step 3 but use cross stitch instead of tent stitch.

**3** Make up the finished fire screen according to the instructions in Chapter 9.

## Size

2 x 2¼in (50 x 57mm)

## Materials

Aida fabric, 18 count: 4in (100mm) square

Stranded cotton embroidery thread as listed in key: approx. 1yd (1m) each

Small rectangular embroidery frame

Tapestry needles: No. 26 or 28

Tacking cotton

PVA wood glue

Flat stripwood, ⅛in (3mm) thick: 2¼ x 2½in (55 x 62mm), 1 piece

Square stripwood, ⅛ x ⅛in (3 x 3mm): 1½in (38mm) long, 1 piece

Miniature picture frame moulding: 12in (300mm), 1 piece

Card: 4in (100mm) square

# Cushion 2

## Size

1¼in (32mm) square

A larger cushion can be made by using a 35 count fabric

## Materials

Evenweave linen, 40 count: 4in (100mm) square

Lightweight fabric for the cushion back: 4in (100mm) square

Stranded cotton embroidery thread as listed in key: approx. 1yd (1m) each

Tacking cotton

Small rectangular embroidery frame or card mount

Tapestry needles: No. 26 or 28

Sewing thread to match cushion

Small amount of wadding or small plastic beads for filling

The bowl of flowers which forms the design for the second cushion in this chapter is based on a design featured in *Weldon's Period Needlework* (No. 5, 1940s). This was a series of magazines with designs looking back to earlier needlework. They included illustrations of historical pieces, together with patterns, charts and transfers for projects for the reader to work. The magazines were not dated, but a good estimate can be made from studying the fashions in the advertisements.

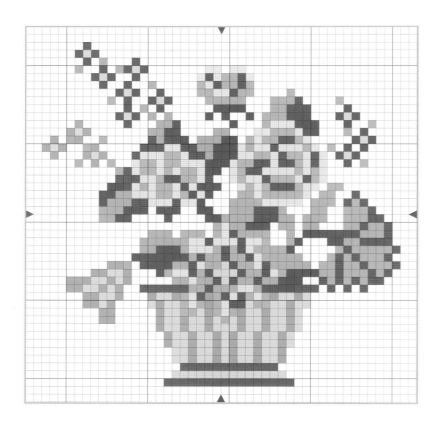

|  |  | DMC | Anchor | Madeira |
|---|---|---|---|---|
|  | Dark pink | 600 | 1006 | 0704 |
|  | Medium pink | 603 | 62 | 0701 |
|  | Light pink | 605 | 60 | 0613 |
|  | Brown | 610 | 889 | 2106 |
|  | Orange | 740 | 316 | 0202 |
|  | Yellow | 725 | 305 | 0106 |
|  | Light blue | 798 | 137 | 0911 |
|  | Medium green | 904 | 258 | 1413 |
|  | Light green | 907 | 255 | 1410 |

## Working method

**1** Mount the fabric into a small embroidery frame or card mount and mark the vertical and horizontal centres with tacking cotton.

**2** Refer to the chart, and begin working from the centre. Each square on the chart represents one stitch over one thread of the linen. Use one strand of stranded cotton and tent stitch throughout.

**3** When the embroidery is complete remove from the frame.

**4** Make up the cushion as directed in Chapter 9.

# Jacobean Bedcover

A selection of autumnal colours has been used for this project and the rug on pages 66–67. The bedcover is of a square design and could be adapted for a cushion, on a smaller-count fabric, or a fire screen on the 35 count used here. A wall hanging could be achieved on a larger count of 24 or 28.

## Working method

**1** Mount the fabric into a small rectangular embroidery frame and mark the vertical and horizontal centres with tacking stitches.

**2** Referring to the chart, begin working near the centre; each square on the chart represents one stitch over one thread of the linen. Use one strand of stranded cotton and tent stitch the main design.

### Size

Design size: 2⅛in (54mm) square

Border: 4in (100mm) square

Bedcover: 6in (150mm) square, or as desired

### Materials

Evenweave linen, 35 count: 8in (200mm) square

Lightweight Habutai silk or cotton lawn for lining: 8in (200mm) square

Stranded cotton embroidery thread as listed in key: approx. 1yd (1m) each

Square embroidery frame

Tacking cotton

Tapestry needles: No. 26 or 28

Sewing thread to match fabric

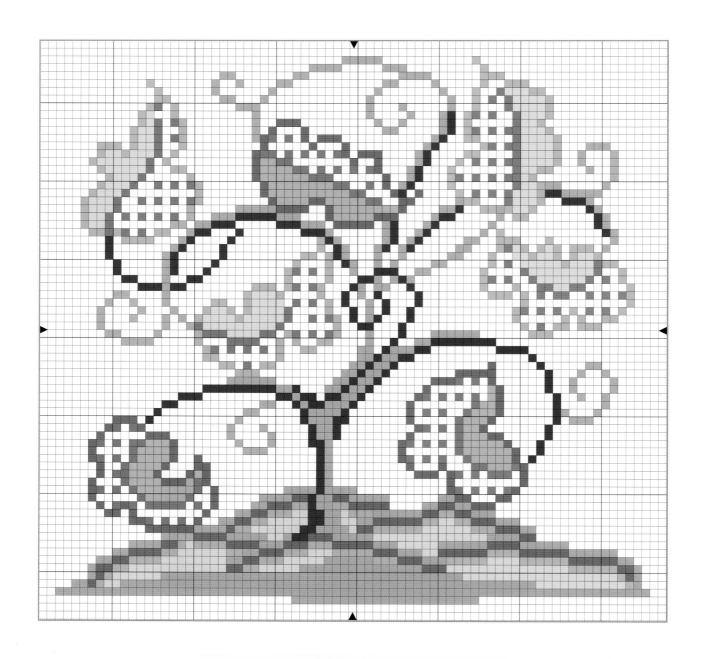

| | | DMC | Anchor | Madeira |
|---|---|---|---|---|
| | Dark brown | 610 | 889 | 2106 |
| | Light brown | 612 | 888 | 2108 |
| | Yellow | 725 | 305 | 0106 |
| | Blue | 807 | 168 | 1109 |
| | Light orange | 741 | 314 | 0201 |
| | Dark orange | 921 | 1003 | 0311 |

**3** When the embroidery of the main design is complete, measure a 4in (100mm) square around it and work four rows of running stitch in colours from the main motif. The running stitch is then counted, over two threads and under two threads of the fabric. You may also refer to the photograph on page 63 as a guide.

**4** When the embroidery is complete remove from the frame.

**5** Make up the bedcover as directed in Chapter 9.

# Jacobean Rug

This semi-circular rug is typical of the shape used during the 1930s and 40s. The colours complement the bedcover (see pages 63–65).

## Size

4½ x 2¼in (115 x 57mm)

## Materials

Single thread canvas, 24 count: 6 x 4in (150 x 100mm)

Stranded cotton embroidery thread as listed in key: approx. 1yd (1m) each. ½ skein for background colour

Tacking thread

Small rectangular embroidery frame

Tapestry needles: No. 26 or 28

## Working method

**1** Mount the fabric into a small embroidery frame and mark the vertical and horizontal centres with tacking stitches.

**2** Refer to Chapter 9 for the method for finishing the edges of the rug. The third row in

| | | DMC | Anchor | Madeira |
|---|---|---|---|---|
| | Dark brown | 610 | 889 | 2106 |
| | Light brown | 612 | 888 | 2108 |
| | Yellow | 725 | 305 | 0106 |
| | Blue | 807 | 168 | 1109 |
| | Light orange | 741 | 314 | 0201 |
| | Dark orange | 921 | 1003 | 0311 |
| | Background cream | 677 | 886 | 2207 |

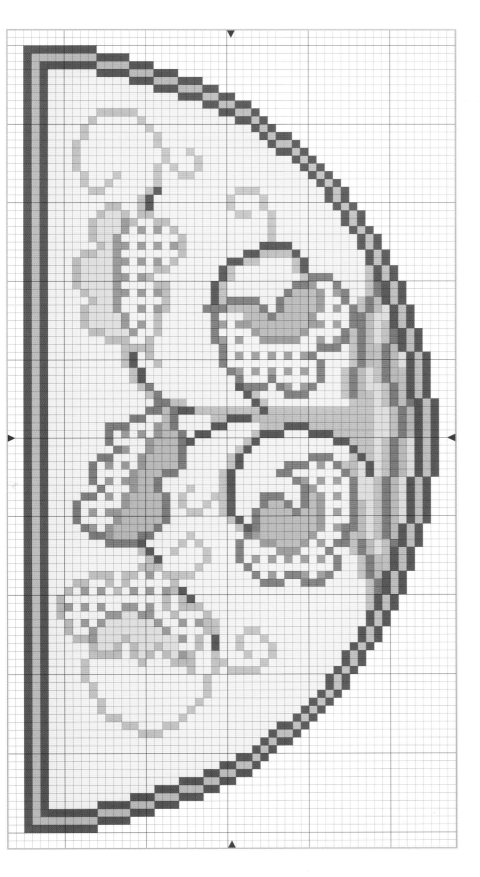

from the straight edge is not initially worked. This forms part of the hem on the straight edge. Therefore, do not work these stitches until the rug is being made up.

**3** Refer to the chart, and begin to work from the centre. Each square on the chart represents one stitch over one thread of the canvas. Use two strands of stranded cotton and tent stitch throughout.

**4** When the embroidery is complete remove from the frame. If the rug has distorted, you may need to block the canvas back into shape. This must be done before the edges are turned under. Instructions for this process are in Chapter 9.

**5** Complete the edges and finish as directed in Chapter 10.

# 5

# Crinoline Ladies and Cottage Gardens

Two of the most popular design themes for embroiderers from the 1930s until the late 1950s was the combination of a lady in a crinoline dress within a cottage garden, and the cottage garden with or without the cottage.

The crinoline lady was a favourite as she was always shown side face, so that the bonnet hid the face completely. Also, the hands were hidden behind a posy of flowers, a basket of flowers or in a muff. Therefore, all the difficult areas did not have to be stitched.

The cottage garden usually included hollyhocks worked as a circle of buttonhole stitch with French knots in the centre; roses worked with rounded, overlapping bullion knots; daisies consisting of radiating straight stitches with knotted centres; and anonymous flowers in detached chain stitch, known as 'lazy daisy'.

Most of the items used were household linen: tea cosies, tray cloths, dressing-table sets, chair backs and table runners. Cushions were also a great favourite and showed the more pictorial designs.

# Picture: Through the Garden Gate

This design is based on the cover of Weldon's needle-art series, *Flower Embroidery*. It is undated but, from the fashions in the advertisements, would seem to be mid-1940s. Looking through a gate was a popular design viewpoint, as were the flower beds backed with tall hollyhocks and wisteria.

## Size

1⅝ x 1½in (40 x 38mm)

## Materials

Evenweave linen, 40 count: 4in (100mm) square

Stranded cotton embroidery thread as listed in key: approx. 1yd (1m) each

Tacking cotton

Small rectangular embroidery frame

Tapestry needles: No. 26 or 28

12in (300mm) miniature picture frame moulding

100mm (4in) square thin card

PVA glue

| | | DMC | Anchor | Madeira |
|---|---|---|---|---|
|  | Dark grey | 413 | 236 | 1713 |
| | Light grey | 762 | 234 | 1804 |
| | Dark olive green | 730 | 924 | 1614 |
| | Mid olive green | 732 | 281 | 1613 |
| | Light olive green | 734 | 280 | 1610 |
| | Dark brown | 610 | 889 | 2106 |
| | Light brown | 612 | 888 | 2108 |
| | Cream | 677 | 886 | 2207 |
| | Dark mauve | 553 | 99 | 0712 |
| | Light mauve | 554 | 96 | 0711 |
| | Red | 666 | 9046 | 0210 |
| | Orange | 741 | 314 | 0201 |
| | Yellow | 725 | 305 | 0106 |
| | Dark pink | 892 | 28 | 0412 |
| | Light pink | 776 | 24 | 0607 |
| | Dark blue | 799 | 145 | 0910 |
| | Light blue | 800 | 159 | 1002 |
| | Rust | 921 | 1003 | 0311 |
| | Salmon | 758 | 882 | 0403 |

## Working method

**1**  Mount the fabric into a small embroidery frame and mark the vertical and horizontal centres with tacking stitches. These can be removed once a few embroidery stitches have been worked.

**2**  Refer to the chart, and begin working from the centre. Each square on the chart represents one stitch over one thread of the canvas. Use one strand of stranded cotton and tent stitch throughout.

**3**  When the embroidery is complete, remove from the frame.

**4**  Mount and frame the embroidery according to the instructions given in Chapter 9.

# Picture: Tudor Cottage

Here is a smaller picture, showing a country cottage, behind a picket fence with an abundant display of colourful flowers.

## Size

1¼ x 1½in (32 x 38mm)

## Materials

Evenweave linen, 40 count: 4in (100mm) square

Stranded cotton embroidery thread as listed in key: approx. 1yd (1m) each

Tacking cotton

Small rectangular embroidery frame

Tapestry needles: No. 26 or 28

12in (300mm) miniature picture frame moulding

4in (100mm) square thin card

PVA glue

|  |  | DMC | Anchor | Madeira |
|---|---|---|---|---|
|  | Black | 310 | Black | Black |
|  | White | Blanc | White | White |
|  | Dark green | 937 | 268 | 1504 |
|  | Mid green | 906 | 256 | 1412 |
|  | Light green | 907 | 255 | 1410 |
|  | Dark brown | 610 | 889 | 2106 |
|  | Light brown | 612 | 888 | 2108 |
|  | Cream | 677 | 886 | 2207 |
|  | Dark mauve | 553 | 99 | 0712 |
|  | Light mauve | 554 | 96 | 0711 |
|  | Red | 666 | 9046 | 0210 |
|  | Orange | 741 | 314 | 0201 |
|  | Yellow | 725 | 305 | 0106 |
|  | Dark pink | 892 | 28 | 0412 |
|  | Light pink | 776 | 24 | 0607 |
|  | Dark blue | 799 | 145 | 0910 |
|  | Light blue | 800 | 159 | 1002 |

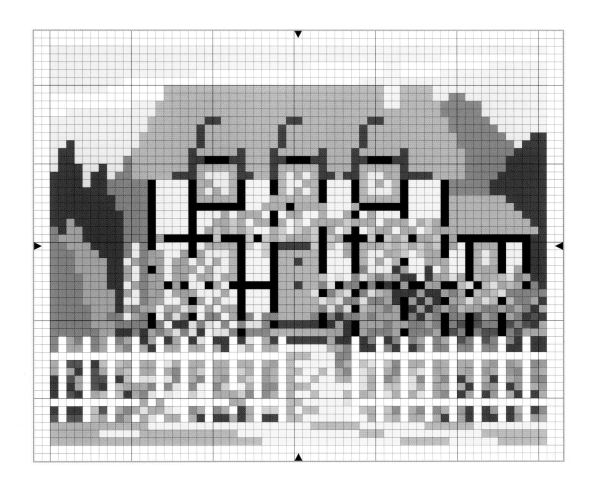

## Working method

1   Mount the fabric into a small embroidery frame and mark the vertical and horizontal centres with tacking stitches. These can be removed once a few embroidery stitches have been worked.

2   Refer to the chart, and begin working from the centre. Each square on the chart represents one stitch over one thread of the canvas. Use one strand of stranded cotton and tent stitch throughout.

3   When the embroidery is complete, remove from the frame.

4   Mount and frame the embroidery according to the instructions given in Chapter 9.

# Picture:
# Blue Lady

A typical view of a crinoline lady walking in a garden is featured in this design.

The rectangular shape would also be appropriate for use as a fire screen.

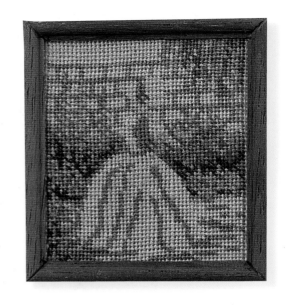

## Size

1½ x 1¼in (38 x 32mm)

## Materials

Evenweave linen, 40 count: 4in (100mm) square

Stranded cotton embroidery thread as listed in key: approx. 1yd (1m) each

Tacking cotton

Small rectangular embroidery frame

Tapestry needles: No. 26 or 28

12in (300mm) miniature picture frame moulding

4in (100mm) square thin card

PVA glue

|  |  | DMC | Anchor | Madeira |
|---|---|---|---|---|
|  | Dark green | 937 | 268 | 1504 |
|  | Mid green | 905 | 257 | 1412 |
|  | Light green | 907 | 255 | 1410 |
|  | Light brown | 612 | 888 | 2108 |
|  | Cream | 677 | 886 | 2207 |
|  | Dark mauve | 553 | 99 | 0712 |
|  | Light mauve | 554 | 96 | 0711 |
|  | Red | 666 | 9046 | 0210 |
|  | Orange | 741 | 314 | 0201 |
|  | Yellow | 725 | 305 | 0106 |
|  | Dark pink | 892 | 28 | 0412 |
|  | Light pink | 776 | 24 | 0607 |
|  | Dark blue | 799 | 145 | 0910 |
|  | Light blue | 800 | 159 | 1002 |

## Working method

**1**   Mount the fabric into a small embroidery frame and mark the vertical and horizontal centres with tacking stitches. These can be removed once a few embroidery stitches have been worked.

**2**   Refer to the chart, and begin working from the centre. Each square on the chart represents one stitch over one thread of the canvas. Use one strand of stranded cotton and tent stitch throughout.

**3**   When the embroidery is complete, remove from the frame.

**4**   Mount and frame the embroidery according to the instructions in Chapter 9.

# Picture or Cushion: Silhouette

## Size

1⅛in (28mm) square

## Materials

Evenweave fabric, 35 count: 4in (100mm) square

Stranded cotton embroidery thread as listed in key: approx. 1yd (1m) each

Tacking cotton

Small embroidery frame

Tapestry needles: No. 26 or 28

As a picture:

    12in (300mm) miniature picture frame moulding

    4in (100mm) square thin card

    PVA glue

As a cushion:

    4in (100mm) square lightweight fabric for the cushion back

    Sewing thread to match

    Small amount of wadding or small plastic beads for filling.

This simple design, based on the silhouette of a crinoline lady, can be used for a picture or for a cushion. However, the inspiration has been taken from the popular fashion in the 1940s, during the shortages after World War II, for simple foil pictures.

These were composed of a sheet of glass, the back of which was painted black leaving the silhouette of the lady unpainted. A piece of silver or coloured foil was then placed behind the glass, enabling the foil to show through the clear-shaped area. The picture was then framed in a simple narrow frame and displayed on the wall.

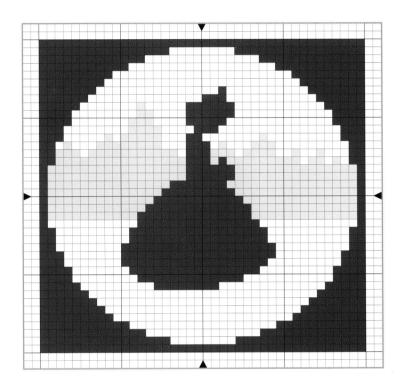

| | | DMC | Anchor | Madeira |
|---|---|---|---|---|
| ▓ | Dark grey | 413 | 236 | 1713 |
| ░ | Light grey | 453 | 231 | 1806 |

## Working method

Dark grey has been used for this project rather than black, as the use of black for miniature work can look very heavy.

**1** Mount the fabric into a small embroidery frame and mark the vertical and horizontal centres with tacking stitches. These can be removed once a few embroidery stitches have been worked.

**2** Refer to the chart, and begin working in the centre. Each square on the chart represents one stitch over one thread of the canvas. Use one strand of embroidery cotton, and tent stitch throughout.

**3** When the embroidery is complete remove from the frame.

**4** Mount and frame the embroidery as a picture as directed in Chapter 9.

**5** Alternatively, make into a cushion according to the instructions given in Chapter 9.

 # Pair of Cushions

These projects encompass the design theme of this chapter, showing the garden, garden gate, and a crinoline lady collecting flowers.

As with many of the square designs in this book, they could also be used for pictures, fire screens or other pieces.

## Size

1¼in (32mm) square

## Materials

Evenweave linen, 35 count: 4in (100mm) square

Lightweight fabric for back of cushion: 4in (100mm) square

Stranded cotton embroidery thread as listed in key: approx. 1yd (1m) each

Tacking cotton

Small embroidery frame

Tapestry needles: No. 26 or 28

Small amount of wadding or small plastic beads for filling

| | | DMC | Anchor | Madeira |
|---|---|---|---|---|
| | Dark red | | | |
| | or colour of choice | 816 | 1005 | 0512 |
| | Light green | 504 | 1042 | 1701 |
| | Mid green | 502 | 876 | 1703 |
| | Dark green | 320 | 216 | 1311 |
| | Light blue | 800 | 159 | 1002 |
| | Dark blue | 799 | 145 | 0910 |
| | Peach | 352 | 9 | 0303 |
| | Pink | 776 | 24 | 0607 |
| | Yellow | 725 | 305 | 0106 |
| | Light brown | 612 | 888 | 2108 |

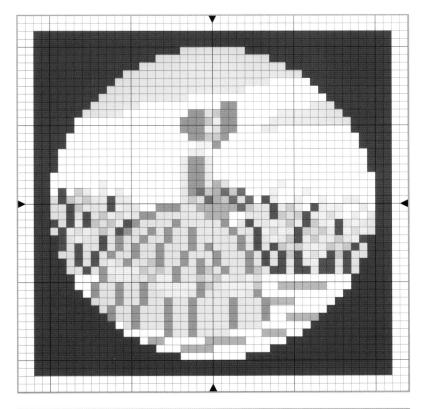

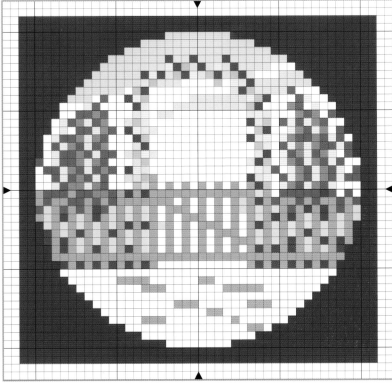

## Working method for both cushions

**1** Mount the fabric into a small embroidery frame and mark the vertical and horizontal centres with tacking stitches. These can be removed once a few embroidery stitches have been worked.

**2** Refer to your desired chart, and begin working from near the centre. Each square on the chart represents one stitch over one thread of the canvas. Use one strand of stranded cotton and tent stitch throughout.

**3** When the embroidery is complete remove from the frame.

**4** Make up the cushion according to the instructions in Chapter 9.

# Tea Cosy

The tea cosy was a familiar object in most homes throughout the twentieth century. They were made in quilted fabric, patchwork, leather, felt, knitted wool; almost every technique you can think of. This miniature example has been worked on silk gauze to cut down the bulk for making up, though an evenweave linen could also be used.

## Working method

**1** Mount the fabric into a small card mount or embroidery frame and mark the vertical and horizontal centres with tacking stitches. These tacking stitches can be removed once a few embroidery stitches have been worked.

**2** Refer to the chart, and begin working near to the centre. Each square on the chart represents one stitch over one thread of the canvas. Use one strand of stranded cotton and tent stitch throughout.

When the embroidery is complete, make up the cosy as follows.

## Size

1⅛ x 1in (28 x 25mm)

## Materials

Silk gauze, 40 count: 2in (50mm) square

*or* evenweave linen, 40 count: 2in (50mm) square

Lightweight fabric for the tea cosy back

Stranded cotton embroidery thread as listed in key: approx. 1yd (1m) each

Tacking cotton

Small card or rectangular embroidery frame

Tapestry needles: No. 26 or 28

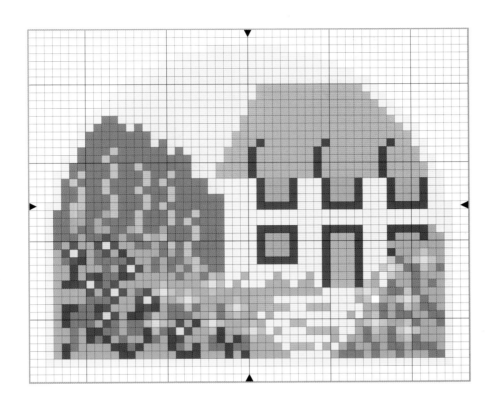

| | | DMC | Anchor | Madeira |
|---|---|---|---|---|
| | Dark blue | 799 | 145 | 0910 |
| | Light blue | 800 | 159 | 1002 |
| | Dark green | 937 | 268 | 1504 |
| | Mid green | 320 | 216 | 1311 |
| | Light green | 907 | 255 | 1410 |
| | Red | 666 | 9046 | 0210 |
| | Orange | 741 | 314 | 0201 |
| | Mauve | 554 | 96 | 0711 |
| | Dark brown | 610 | 889 | 2106 |
| | Light brown | 612 | 888 | 2108 |
| | Cream | 677 | 886 | 2207 |
| | Yellow | 725 | 305 | 0106 |

**4** Add a tiny loop of thread to the top centre edge of the cosy, pointing downwards.

**5** Place the completed embroidery and the fabric for the back right sides together.

**6** Using a very small back stitch, stitch around the curved edge of the embroidery.

**7** Trim the excess fabric away and turn the cosy through to the right side.

**8** Trim the open edges to about ¼in (6mm) and tuck up inside the cosy to the edge of the embroidery. Hold in place with a few stitches.

**9** There is no need for padding as the thickness of the embroidery and the turnings will suffice.

# 6

# Cross Stitch and Samplers

During the whole of the twentieth century, counted thread work and cross stitch were popular with embroiderers. Samplers have been worked in great numbers since the seventeenth century, both as schoolroom exercises and as decorative objects.

Twentieth-century samplers were simpler in design compared to earlier examples, ranging from verses and alphabets, to pictorial representations of houses, flowers, animals and so on.

Cross stitch became very popular due to a revival during the 1950s, after the austerity and shortages of the World War II. In Regent Street, London, the Needlewoman Shop imported designs and prepared kits from Denmark which sold in great numbers. The magazines of the day included many charts and projects. Materials and threads were becoming more widely available and of a better quality while the designs were predominantly floral and were used mainly for household items.

The designs in the these projects can be used for items other than those shown, so do experiment.

# House Sampler

This sampler has a simple border and typical motifs, including a house, crown and animals.

## Size

1¼ x 1½in (32 x 38mm)

## Materials

Evenweave linen, 35 count: 4in (100mm) square

Stranded cotton embroidery thread as listed in key: approx. 1yd (1m) each

Tacking cotton

Small rectangular embroidery frame or card mount

Tapestry needles: No. 26 or 28

Miniature picture frame moulding: 12in (300mm)

Piece of thin card: 4in (100mm) square

PVA glue

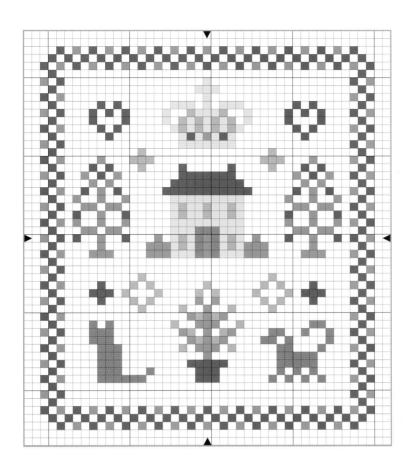

| | | DMC | Anchor | Madeira |
|---|---|---|---|---|
| | Red | 666 | 9046 | 0210 |
| | Green | 906 | 256 | 1410 |
| | Yellow | 725 | 305 | 0106 |
| | Blue | 799 | 145 | 1910 |
| | Brown | 640 | 903 | 1905 |

## Working method

**1** Mount the fabric into a small embroidery frame or card mount and mark the vertical and horizontal centres with tacking stitches. These tacking stitches can be removed once a few embroidery stitches have been worked.

**2** Refer to the chart, and begin working from the centre. Each square on the chart represents one stitch over one thread of the canvas. Use either cross or tent stitch throughout according to your preference, using one strand of stranded cotton.

**3** Avoid taking a dark-coloured thread across the back of the work where a space will not have any stitches as the colour may show through.

**4** Once the house has been worked, the position of the other motifs can easily be found.

**5** Finally work the border.

**6** When the embroidery is complete remove from the frame.

**7** Mount and frame the sampler according to the instructions given in Chapter 9.

# Home Sweet Home Sampler

This sampler incorporates some backstitch lettering within a simple border and with a popular motto.

### Size

1⅜ x 1⅝in (35 x 40mm)

### Materials

Evenweave linen, 35 count: 4in (100mm) square

Stranded cotton embroidery thread as listed in key: approx. 1yd (1m) each

Tacking cotton

Small rectangular embroidery frame or card mount

Tapestry needles: No. 26 or 28

Miniature picture frame moulding: 12in (300mm)

Thin card: 4in (100mm) square

PVA glue

## Working method

**1** Mount the fabric into a small embroidery frame or card mount and mark the vertical and horizontal centres with tacking stitches. These tacking stitches can be removed once a few embroidery stitches have been worked.

| | | DMC | Anchor | Madeira |
|---|---|---|---|---|
| | Red | 666 | 9046 | 0210 |
| | Green | 906 | 256 | 1410 |

**2** Refer to the chart, and begin working from the centre. Each square on the chart represents one stitch over one thread of the canvas. The solid coloured squares on the chart indicate either cross or tent stitch throughout according to your preference, using one strand of stranded cotton. The lines within the squares of the chart represent a back stitch worked in the direction indicated by the line.

**3** Avoid taking a dark-coloured thread across the back of the work where a space will not have any stitches as the colour may show through.

**4** Once the motto has been worked, the position of the other motifs and alphabet can be located.

**5** Finally work the border.

**6** When the embroidery is complete remove from the frame.

**7** Mount and frame the sampler according to the instructions given in Chapter 9.

# Reindeer Sampler

A square format has been used for this sampler with a central tree, two reindeer and two exotic birds. The sampler also has a more elaborate border.

## Size

1½in (38mm) square

## Materials

Evenweave linen, 35 count: 4in (100mm) square

Stranded cotton embroidery thread as listed in key: approx. 1yd (1m) each

Tacking cotton

Small rectangular embroidery frame or card mount

Tapestry needles: No. 26 or 28

Miniature picture frame moulding: 12in (300mm)

PVA glue

## Working method

**1** Mount the fabric into a small embroidery frame or card mount and mark the vertical and horizontal centres with tacking stitches. These tacking stitches can be removed once a few embroidery stitches have been worked.

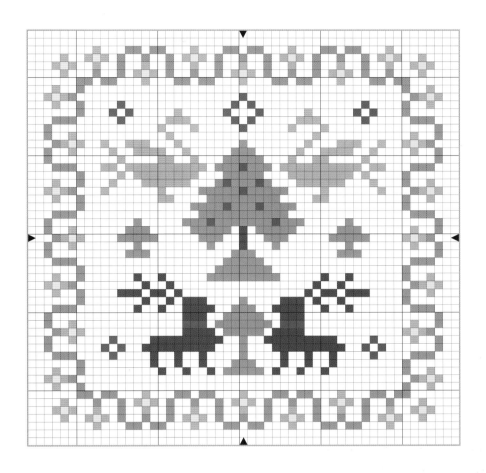

| | | DMC | Anchor | Madeira |
|---|---|---|---|---|
| | Red | 666 | 9046 | 0210 |
| | Green | 906 | 256 | 1410 |
| | Yellow | 725 | 305 | 0106 |
| | Blue | 799 | 145 | 0910 |
| | Brown | 610 | 889 | 2106 |

**2** Refer to the chart, and begin working from the centre. Each square on the chart represents one stitch over one thread of the canvas. Use either cross or tent stitch throughout according to your preference, using one strand of stranded cotton.

**3** Avoid taking a dark-coloured thread across the back of the work where a space will not have any stitches as the colour may show through.

**4** Once the central tree has been worked, the position of the other motifs can easily be found.

**5** Finally work the border.

**6** When the embroidery is complete remove from the frame.

**7** Mount and frame the sampler according to the instructions given in Chapter 9.

# Peacock Sampler

### Size

1½in (38mm) square

### Materials

Evenweave linen, 35 count: 4in (100mm) square

Stranded cotton embroidery thread as listed in key: approx. 1yd (1m) each

Tacking cotton

Small rectangular embroidery frame or card mount

Tapestry needles: No. 26 or 28

Miniature picture frame moulding: 12in (300mm)

PVA glue

### Working method

**1**   Mount the fabric into a small embroidery frame or card mount and mark the vertical and horizontal centres with tacking stitches. These tacking stitches can be removed once a few embroidery stitches have been worked.

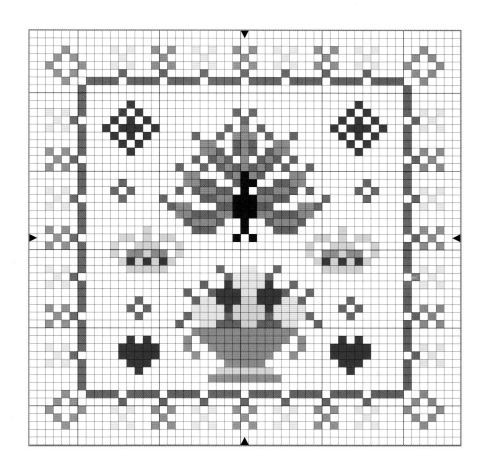

|  |  | DMC | Anchor | Madeira |
|---|---|---|---|---|
|  | Red | 666 | 9046 | 0210 |
|  | Green | 906 | 256 | 1410 |
|  | Yellow | 725 | 305 | 0106 |
|  | Blue | 799 | 145 | 0910 |
|  | Brown | 610 | 889 | 2106 |
|  | Pink | 776 | 24 | 0607 |

**2**  Refer to the chart, and begin working from the centre. Each square on the chart represents one stitch over one thread of the canvas. Use either cross or tent stitch throughout according to your preference, using one strand of stranded cotton.

**3**  Avoid taking a dark-coloured thread across the back of the work where a space will not have any stitches as the colour may show through.

**4**  Once the central tree has been worked, the position of the other motifs can easily be found.

**5**  Finally work the border.

**6**  When the embroidery is complete remove from the frame.

**7**  Mount and frame the sampler according to the instructions given in Chapter 9.

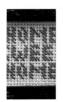

# Small Motto Samplers

## Size

1 x ⅝in (25 x 15mm)

## Materials

Enough for three samplers:

Evenweave linen, 35 count: 5in (126mm) square

Stranded cotton embroidery thread as listed in key: approx. 1yd (1m) each

Tacking cotton

Small rectangular embroidery frame or card mount

Tapestry needles: No. 26 or 28

Stripwood: ⅛ x ⅛ x 12in (3 x 3 x 300mm)

Piece of thin card: 5in (126mm) square

PVA glue

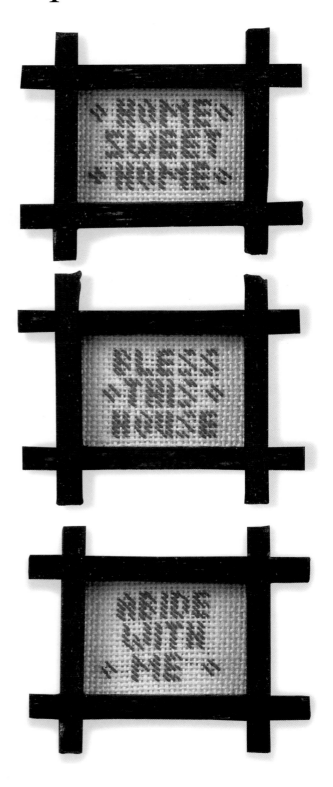

## Working method

**1** Mount the fabric in a small embroidery frame or card mount. These three samplers are small, so can be worked together with a space in between.

**2** There is no need to mark the vertical and horizontal centres with tacking stitches.

**3** Refer to the chart; each square represents one stitch over one thread of the canvas. Use either cross or tent stitch throughout according to your preference, using one strand of stranded cotton.

**4** When the embroidery is complete remove from the frame.

**5** Mount and frame the samplers according to the instructions given in Chapter 9, using stripwood.

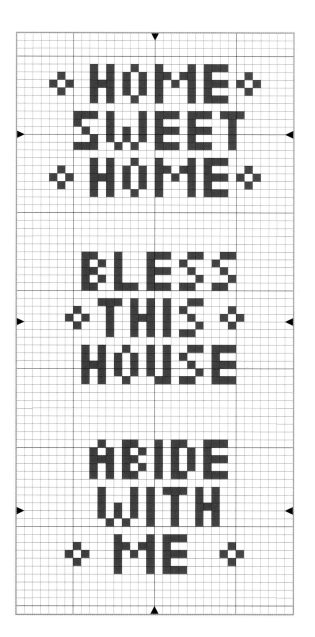

| | DMC | Anchor | Madeira |
|---|---|---|---|
| Red or colour of choice | 666 | 9046 | 0210 |

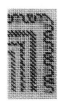

# Design and Create your own Sampler

To facilitate the designing of your own individual samplers, I have included a series of charts showing alphabets, motifs and borders.

Samplers come in a variety of sizes. Here are some suggestions:

| FULL SIZE | 1/12 SCALE | 1/24 SCALE |
|---|---|---|
| 12 x 9in (305 x 229mm) | 1 x ¾in (25 x 20mm) | ½ x ⅜in (12 x 10mm) |
| 15 x 12in (381 x 305mm) | 1¼ x 1in (32 x 25mm) | ⅝ x ½in (16 x 12mm) |
| 18 x 12in (457 x 305mm) | 1½ x 1in (38 x 25mm) | ¾ x ½in (19 x 12mm) |
| 21 x 15in (533 x 381mm) | 1¾ x 1¼in (45 x 32mm) | ⅞ x ⅝in (22 x 16mm) |

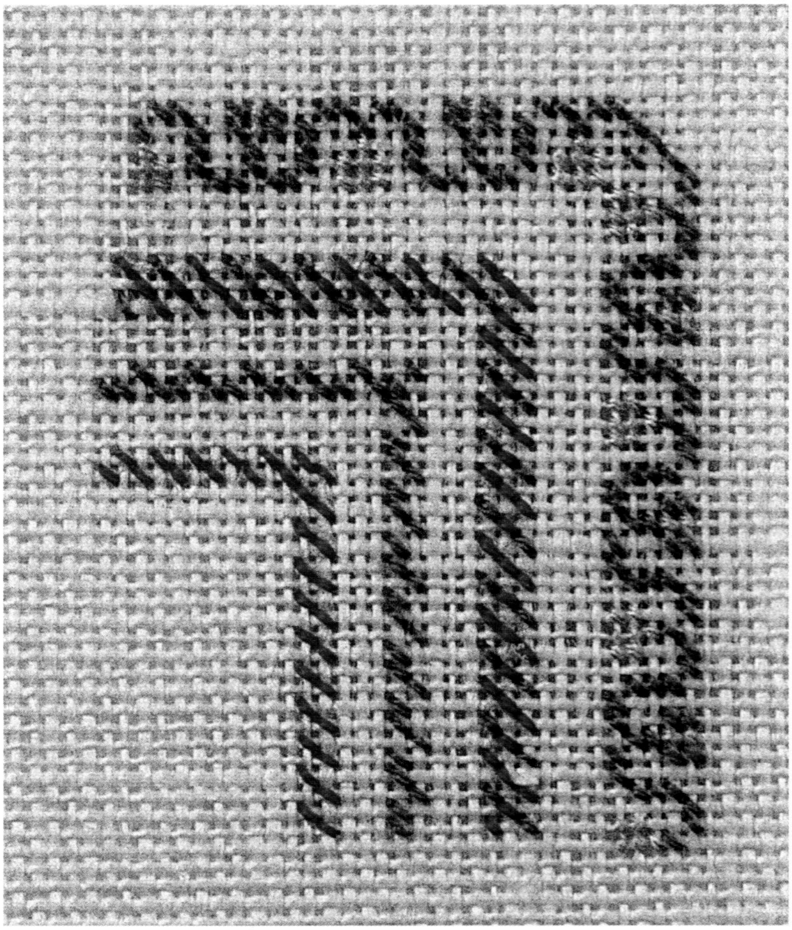

**Assorted borders**

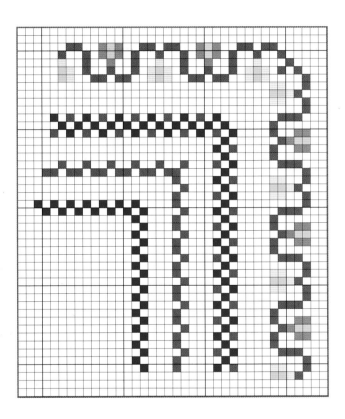

| Suggested colours | DMC | Anchor | Madeira |
|---|---|---|---|
| Red | 666 | 9046 | 0210 |
| Green | 906 | 256 | 1410 |
| Yellow | 725 | 305 | 0106 |
| Blue | 799 | 145 | 0910 |
| Pink | 776 | 24 | 0607 |

The first thing to consider is whether you are working to the size of a ready-made frame, or wish to make your own to a desired size.

## Using a ready-made frame

**1** Measure the inside edges of the frame to find the height and width of the required embroidered area.

**2** Work the border of the sampler first.

**3** Begin the border in the centre of a side and work towards a corner. As you approach the corner you will be aware of where the corner needs to turn. Work one vertical and one horizontal side. If necessary, design a small motif for each corner.

**4** Copy the two worked sides on the remaining vertical and horizontal sides.

**5** Now place your motifs as directed later in this chapter (pages 97–98).

## Using a frame made to size

**1** Decide on the size required.

**2** Work the border first. This time you can begin with a corner and turn the next corner when the desired width or height has been reached. There is some flexibility as the frame can be made to fit the embroidered area.

**3** When the border is complete, the other features of the sampler can be worked, using the directions on the following pages.

# Using Alphabets and Mottos

The next thing to consider when designing your own samplers is whether you wish to include lettering. If so, proceed as follows:

**1** Select a lettering style: the chart shows three forms; a small backstitch version two threads high; a taller backstitch version four threads high; and a tent or cross stitch version, also four threads high.

**2** Write out the desired motto or alphabet, including spaces between words. This is easier if planned out on graph paper.

**3** Count how many squares are used and find the centre. At this point you may need to move some words on to additional lines.

**4** On your sampler, check that you have the required number of threads available.

**5** Place your lettering in the upper or lower half of the sampler, not right in the middle. This will make it easier to position the remaining motifs.

**6** Normally the lettering is centred on the sampler: begin stitching the letter that is nearest to the vertical centre and work to the end of the word or line. Then return to the centre and work the rest of the lettering to the other end of the line.

**7** Complete any lettering.

**A selection of alphabets**

# Positioning the Motifs

The picture below shows a selection of popular motifs of various sizes for use on your samplers.

**1**   The most dominant motifs must be considered first as they probably need to be positioned on the vertical centre line, either above or below the horizontal centre.

**2**   If you place a large motif in the absolute centre, it will seem to be closer to the lower edge, and will spoil the balance of the sampler. This is an optical illusion and applies to all presentation methods.

**3**   When the position of the main motifs has been set, balance them by adding smaller motifs in the spaces. Refer to some of the samplers in the earlier section of this chapter for examples.

The general working instructions and materials for samplers apply as given for the projects.

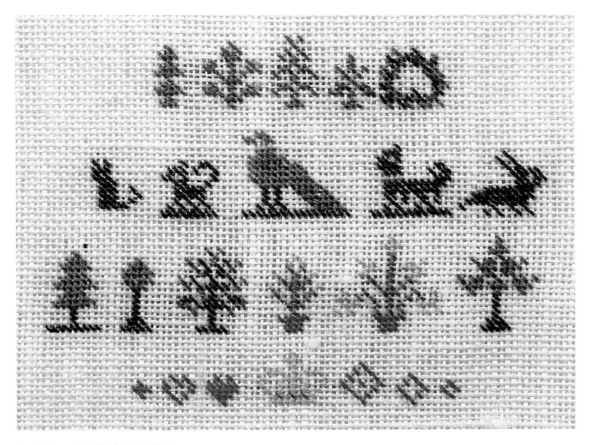

**A selection of motifs for samplers**

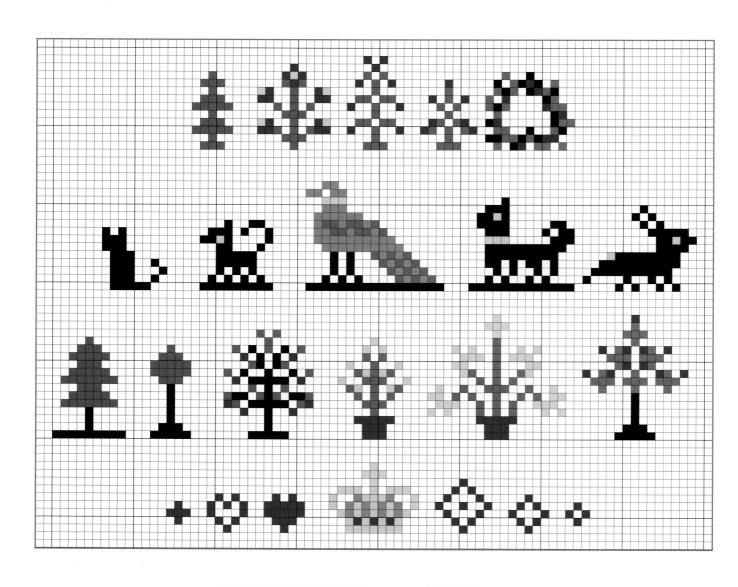

| | | DMC | Anchor | Madeira |
|---|---|---|---|---|
| | Red | 666 | 9046 | 0210 |
| | Green | 906 | 256 | 1410 |
| | Blue | 799 | 145 | 0910 |
| | Yellow | 725 | 305 | 0106 |
| | Dark green | 319 | 683 | 1313 |
| | Brown | 610 | 889 | 2106 |
| | Pink | 3326 | 36 | 0606 |

# Versatile Cross Stitch

Cross stitch will always be a popular technique for embroiderers as it is suitable for all abilities, from complete beginner to expert. Success is assured when a few simple rules are considered:

- When using cross stitch, always have the top stitch of the cross in the same direction.
- Always use a quality evenweave or Aida-type fabric with a true square weave.
- Always use a tapestry needle that will not pierce the threads of the fabric.

The following projects show the typical flower motifs in use throughout the twentieth century. They are suited to many items as the designs are virtually square, and the size can be varied by using different counts of fabric.

# Floral Fire Screen and Cushions

## Cushions

### Size

1⅛ to 1⅝in (28 to 40mm) square, as desired

### Materials

Evenweave linen, 32 count: 4in (100mm) square

Lightweight fabric for cushion back: 4in (100mm) square

Stranded cotton embroidery thread as listed in keys: approx. 1yd (1m) each

Tacking cotton

Small rectangular embroidery frame

Tapestry needles: No. 26 or 28

Small amount of wadding or small plastic beads for filling

### Working method for fire screen and cushions

1 Mount the fabric into a small embroidery frame or card mount and mark the vertical and horizontal centres with tacking stitches. These tacking stitches can be removed once a few embroidery stitches have been worked.

2 Refer to the chart, and begin working near the centre. Each square on the chart represents one stitch over one thread of the canvas. Use one strand of stranded cotton and tent or cross stitch throughout depending on your preference.

3 When the embroidery is complete remove from the frame.

4 Make up the fire screen or cushion according to the instructions given in Chapter 9.

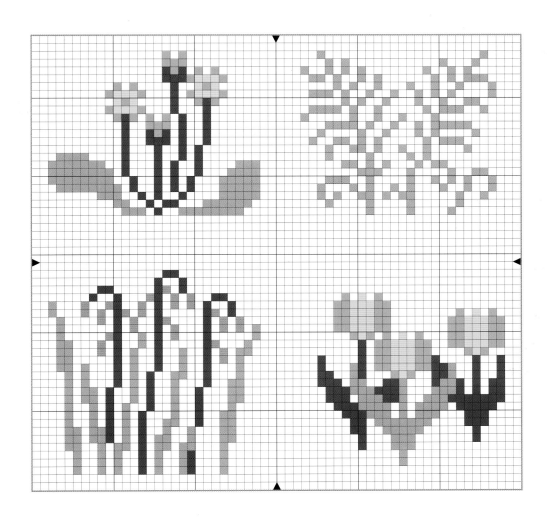

|  | | DMC | Anchor | Madeira |
|---|---|---|---|---|
|  | Orange | 741 | 314 | 0201 |
|  | Yellow | 725 | 305 | 0106 |
|  | Blue | 799 | 145 | 0910 |
|  | Dark green | 905 | 257 | 1412 |
|  | Light green | 907 | 255 | 1410 |

# Fire Screen

This project uses all four of the charts to form a larger embroidered area. Four attractive floral designs are used: the primula, bluebell, tulip and ferns. Refer to the working method on page 100.

## Size

2¼in (57mm) square

## Materials

Evenweave linen, 32 count: 5in (126mm) square

Stranded cotton embroidery thread as listed in keys: approx. 1yd (1m) each

Tacking cotton

Small rectangular embroidery frame

Tapestry needles: No. 26 or 28

Miniature picture frame moulding: 12in (300mm)

Stripwood: ⅛ x ⅛ x 2in (3 x 3 x 50mm)

Piece of card: 4in (100mm) square

PVA glue

# Three More Popular Flower Designs

The following three designs are the most popular from a series published in *The Dolls' House Magazine*, published by GMC Publications, during 2002. They are shown here as cushions but could be used for many items such as, fire screens, folding screens, pole screens, scattered on a rug or bedcover. Working method as for cushions on page 100.

Making up instructions are in Chapter 9.

Making up instructions are in Chapter 9.

**Size**

1⅛ to 1⅝in (28 to 40mm) square, as desired

**Materials**

As for cushions, on page 100. A fabric count of 32, 35 or 40 can be used

Tent stitch using one thread of stranded cotton throughout

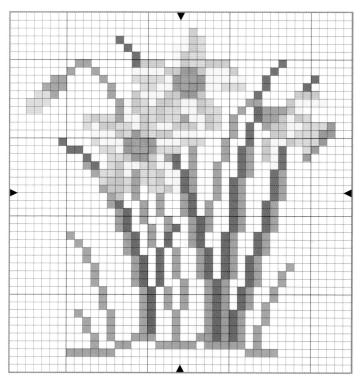

**Daffodil**

**Columbine**

|  | | DMC | Anchor | Madeira |
|---|---|---|---|---|
|  | Dark green | 470 | 266 | 1410 |
|  | Light green | 471 | 255 | 1502 |
|  | Pale yellow | 3078 | 292 | 0102 |
|  | Yellow | 743 | 305 | 0113 |
|  | Pale orange | 402 | 1047 | 2307 |
|  | Orange | 740 | 316 | 0202 |

|  | | DMC | Anchor | Madeira |
|---|---|---|---|---|
|  | Bright pink | 351 | 10 | 0214 |
|  | Mid pink | 353 | 868 | 0304 |
|  | Light pink | 948 | 1011 | 0306 |
|  | Dark green | 470 | 266 | 1410 |
|  | Light green | 471 | 255 | 1502 |
|  | Pale yellow | 3078 | 292 | 0102 |
|  | Yellow | 444 | 297 | 0105 |

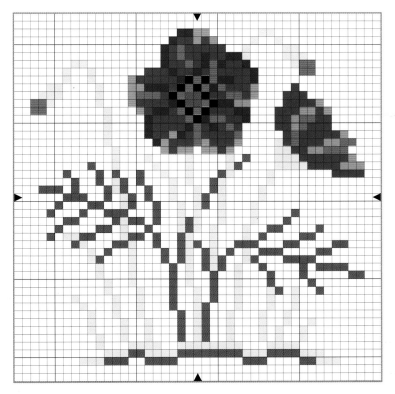

**Poppies**

|  |  | DMC | Anchor | Madeira |
|---|---|---|---|---|
|  | Dark red | 814 | 45 | 0514 |
|  | Med red | 321 | 47 | 0510 |
|  | Bright red | 900 | 332 | 0207 |
|  | Light red | 947 | 330 | 0205 |
|  | Dark green | 502 | 876 | 1703 |
|  | Light green | 504 | 1042 | 1701 |
|  | Black | 311 | Black | Black |

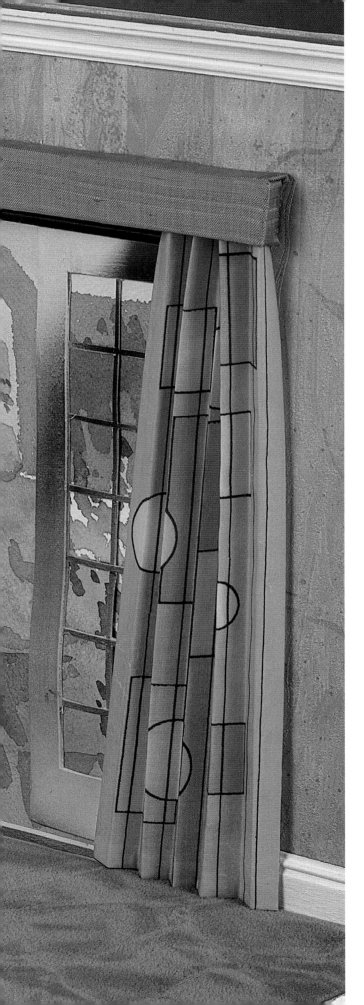

# 7

# Abstract Designs of the 1960s and 70s

During the 1950s, textile and furnishing designs began to use simplified shapes, prompted by magazines of the time, influences such as the American films at the cinema, and exhibitions like the Festival of Britain in 1951.

By the early 1960s many new products and furnishings were becoming available. Although the designs were sometimes the ever-popular flowers, fruit and animals of the earlier decades, the shapes were very simple, often formed with geometric rectangles, circles, ovals, and so on.

The 1960s and 70s saw famous embroiderers such as Beryl Dean and Constance Howard make their mark with fine art pieces. Organizations such as The Women's Institute and Townswomen's Guild maintained the standard of good stitchery, and the Embroiderers' Guild and City and Guilds Institute promoted good needlecraft and design.

During the 1970s students and professional embroiderers alike took the abstract design to an extreme. However, by the 1980s and 90s the pendulum had swung back to the use of good balanced design at all levels.

# Two Modern Cushions

The two cushions pictured below, show the use of simple geometric shapes to create a design typical of the 1960s or 70s. The colours can be changed to suit your own scheme, and the designs can be adapted for use on other items.

## Working method for both cushions

**1**  Mount the fabric into a small embroidery frame or card mount.

**2**  Mark the vertical and horizontal centres with tacking stitches. These can be removed once a few embroidery stitches have been worked.

**3**  Refer to the chart of your chosen design on the following pages, and begin working from the centre. Each square on the chart represents one stitch over one thread of the canvas. Use one strand of stranded cotton and tent stitch throughout.

**4**  It is usually easier to work the motifs first and complete the background after.

**5**  When the embroidery is complete remove from the frame.

**6**  Make up the cushions as directed in Chapter 9.

### Size

1½in (38mm) square

### Materials

Evenweave linen, 35 count: 4in (100mm) square

Lightweight fabric for back of cushion: 4in (100mm) square

Stranded cotton embroidery thread as listed in key: approx. 1yd (1m) each, 4yd (4m) for background colour

Tacking cotton

Small rectangular embroidery frame or card mount

Tapestry needles: No. 26 or 28

Small amount of wadding or small plastic beads for filling

# Cushion 1: Simple Bold Shapes

| | | DMC | Anchor | Madeira |
|---|---|---|---|---|
| | Dark orange | 921 | 1003 | 0311 |
| | Orange | 741 | 314 | 0201 |
| | Yellow | 725 | 305 | 0106 |
| | Grey | 451 | 233 | 1808 |
| | Turquoise | 3811 | 168 | 1109 |

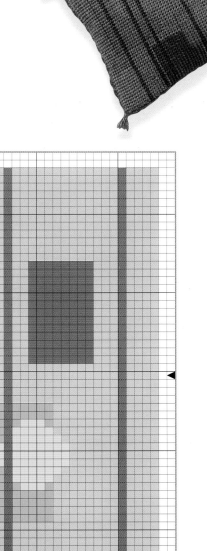

# Cushion 2: Floating Ovals

| | | DMC | Anchor | Madeira |
|---|---|---|---|---|
| | Bright orange | 921 | 1003 | 0311 |
| | Orange | 741 | 314 | 0201 |
| | Yellow | 725 | 305 | 0106 |
| | Turquoise | 3811 | 168 | 1109 |

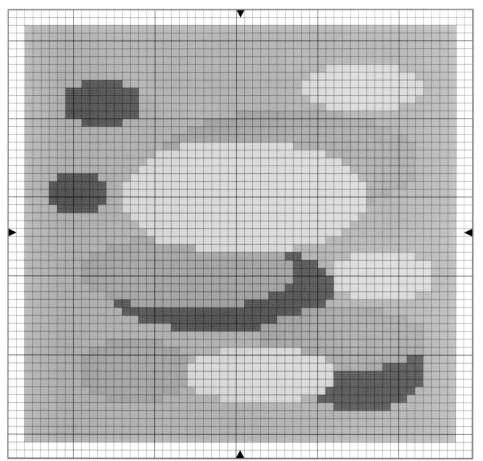

# Hearts Cushion

A very simple little cushion with heart motifs. The heart could be substituted with any small motif. Simply position the desired motif in place of the hearts, then work the diagonal lines and background.

## Working method

**1** Mount the fabric into a small embroidery frame or card mount and mark the vertical and horizontal centres with tacking stitches. These tacking stitches

### Size

1¼in (32mm) square

### Materials

Evenweave linen, 35 count: 4in (100mm) square.

Lightweight fabric for back of cushion: 4in (100mm) square

Stranded cotton embroidery thread as listed in key: approx. 1yd (1m) each, 4yd (4m) for background colour

Tacking cotton

Small rectangular embroidery frame or card mount

Tapestry needles: No. 26 or 28

Small amount of wadding or small plastic beads for filling

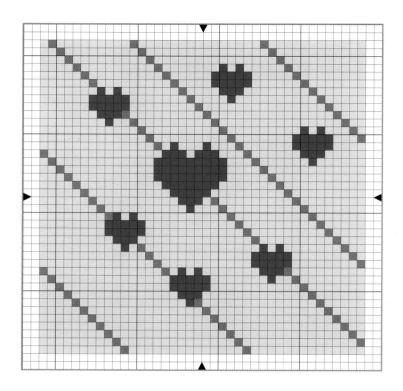

| | | DMC | Anchor | Madeira |
|---|---|---|---|---|
| | Red | 666 | 9046 | 0210 |
| | Dark grey | 451 | 233 | 1808 |
| | Light grey | 453 | 231 | 2806 |

can be removed once a few embroidery stitches have been worked.

**2** Refer to the chart, and begin working from the centre. Each square on the chart represents one stitch over one thread of the canvas. Use one strand of stranded cotton and tent stitch throughout.

**3** It is usually easier to work the motifs first and complete the background after.

**4** When the embroidery is complete remove from the frame.

**5** Make up the cushions according to the instructions given in Chapter 9.

# Curtains

In the typical house of the twentieth century, most curtain arrangements were simple: invariably panels were just hung under a pelmet. This section shows you how to go about making designs for curtains of this type. If more elaborate arrangments are required, a full range of shapes and drapes are included in one of my earlier volumes of this series, *Miniature Embroidery for the Victorian Dolls' House* (also published by GMC Publications).

## Making curtains from bought fabrics

- Purchase fabric woven with a natural fibre if possible, either lightweight cotton or silk; synthetic fabrics do not pleat or gather well.

- For each curtain panel you will need a piece the length of the window plus ½in (12mm). The curtain may only hang to the sill or could be down to floor level.

- 3in (75mm) is usually right for the width of the curtain. Add ½in (12mm) to each side for hems.
- Use the ½in (12mm) to turn a small hem at the lower edge. Either stitch or use PVA glue sparingly, according to your preference.
- Next, hem or glue the side edges.
- Gather and complete the curtains and pelmets as directed in Chapter 9.

## Colouring your own fabrics for curtains

I have provided some simple black and white designs, to match the cushions, for curtains. By tracing off or photocopying the designs they can be coloured to your requirements with fabric transfer paints. This allows the design to be ironed onto fabric which can then be made up. Full details of using fabric transfer paints are given in Chapter 10.

The coloured designs can be scanned into a PC using any graphics or drawing software, and printed off on to special transfer paper. This can then be ironed onto fabric and the colour transferred ready to be made up.

Follow the instructions accompanying the brand of paper you buy.

## Designing your own fabrics and curtains in Microsoft Word

The drawing tools in Word allow designs to be created very simply and quickly and multiple copies can be made with little effort. The AutoShapes give a range of usable simple motifs which, when multiplied or overlapped, create a range of designs suited to miniature work. This process can also be done in very straightforward draw programs, but the options may be more limited.

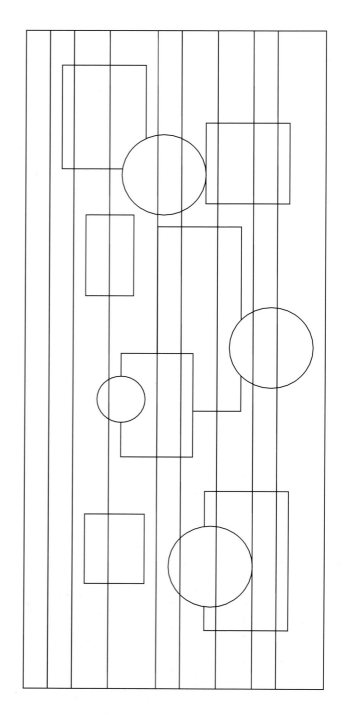

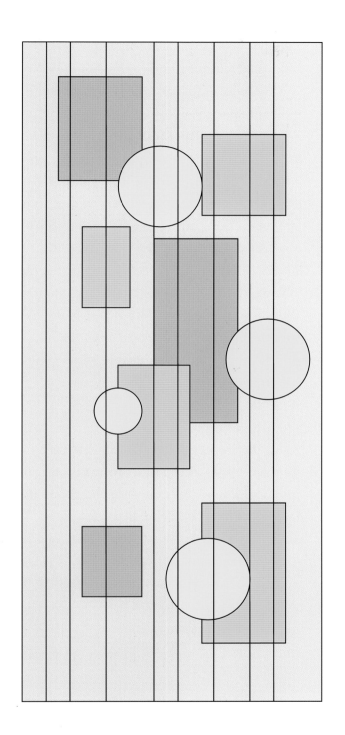

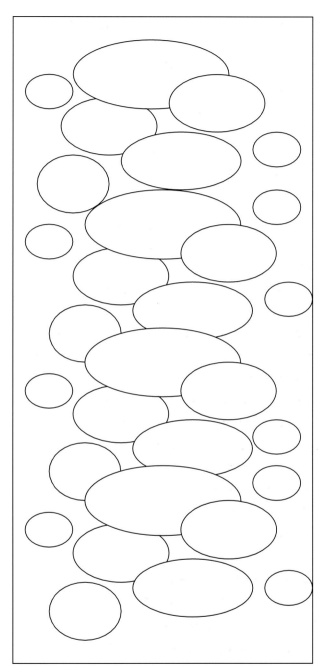

First, ensure that your Drawing toolbar is showing. To do this: click **View**, select **Toolbars**, and from the drop-down menu, make sure that **Drawing** is ticked.

Now, open a new document in Word — **File**, **Open**.

- The **Drawing** toolbar is usually along the lower edge of the screen.

- Click the empty **Rectangle**; a grey rectangle will appear on your document saying **Create drawing here**. The cursor turns into an upright cross.

- Use the **Ruler** bars to judge the size, these are found along the top- and left-hand side of the work area.

- Position the cursor in the top left-hand corner and drag diagonally until the rectangle is about 3in (75mm) wide and about 7in (180mm) long; this is for a curtain. You can fill a page if designing a piece of fabric for other uses.

- Your designated area will now have '**handles**' with which you can change the shape or size by placing the cursor on a point, when it will change to a double-headed arrow, and drag to a new position. You can re-select an object or shape by **left clicking** on it at any time, in order to alter, move or edit it.

- Select a desired shape or line from the **Drawing** toolbar. By selecting the tiny arrow beside **AutoShapes** an additional menu appears, offering a whole range of options.

- Click and drag into position within your defined area. For a line click and hold where it is to start, move the cursor to where it will finish and let go when in the desired place. Each

addition will be '**selected**' with '**handles**' and, while selected, can be moved or edited.

- To **delete** an unwanted shape, select and press the **backspace** key.

- When using the **Rectangle** or **Oval** options, if you need a perfect square or circle, hold down the **Shift** key while dragging into shape.

- Select each element individually and drag into place. Any earlier shape or line can be re-selected by **Left** clicking on the object.

- To repeat a design; select **Copy** from the **Standard** toolbar, place the cursor in the position where the copy is to appear, and select **Paste** from the **Standard** toolbar. The image will then appear. This can then be selected by a left click and moved or edited if necessary.

To colour your design:

- Select the shape to be coloured (**Left** click on the shape), and select **Fill Colour** (a paint pot with a coloured line underneath), from the **Drawing** toolbar. Click the tiny arrow beside the paint pot and a colour palette will appear. Click on the required colour and your shape will fill with that colour.

- Select each area to be coloured in turn and repeat as often as required.

- Finally, select the background areas and repeat.

Save your design at various times during this process, either to the hard disk or a floppy disk. Remember to name it for future reference.

117

# 8

# The Influence of Ethnic Textiles

As the twentieth century progressed, travel became more widespread and available to all. By the 1950s and 60s the package holiday had become standard and, eventually, travel to far-off places not uncommon.

The exotic designs and artefacts of India and the Far East began to filter back to decorate the home. The bright colours and unfamiliar designs were an immediate attraction. The gentler, but exotic, textiles from China were used to adorn many an interior.

Many of the items brought back from travels and holidays were, in fact, made for that purpose and to the taste of the European market while retaining the essence of the country of origin.

The following projects represent the type of designs used for cushions and wall hangings that were popular with tourists and were eventually imported to be sold to the home market.

# Chinese Carpet

The colours used for this project reflect the soft shades of imported Chinese rugs and carpets. The colours can be altered according to your taste, and the size can be adjusted at the plain area between the motifs.

## Size

4½ x 3in (115 x 75mm)

## Materials

Coin net or mono (single-thread) canvas, 24 count: 6 x 5in (150 x 126mm)

Stranded cotton embroidery thread as listed in key: approx. 1yd (1m) each. 1 skein for background colour

Tacking cotton

Small rectangular embroidery frame

Tapestry needles: No. 26 or 28

| | | DMC | Anchor | Madeira |
|---|---|---|---|---|
| | Rust | 356 | 1013 | 0402 |
| | Dark peach | 352 | 9 | 0303 |
| | Light peach | 353 | 868 | 0304 |
| | Flesh | 950 | 376 | 2309 |
| | Light flesh | 951 | 880 | 2308 |
| | Olive green | 734 | 280 | 1610 |

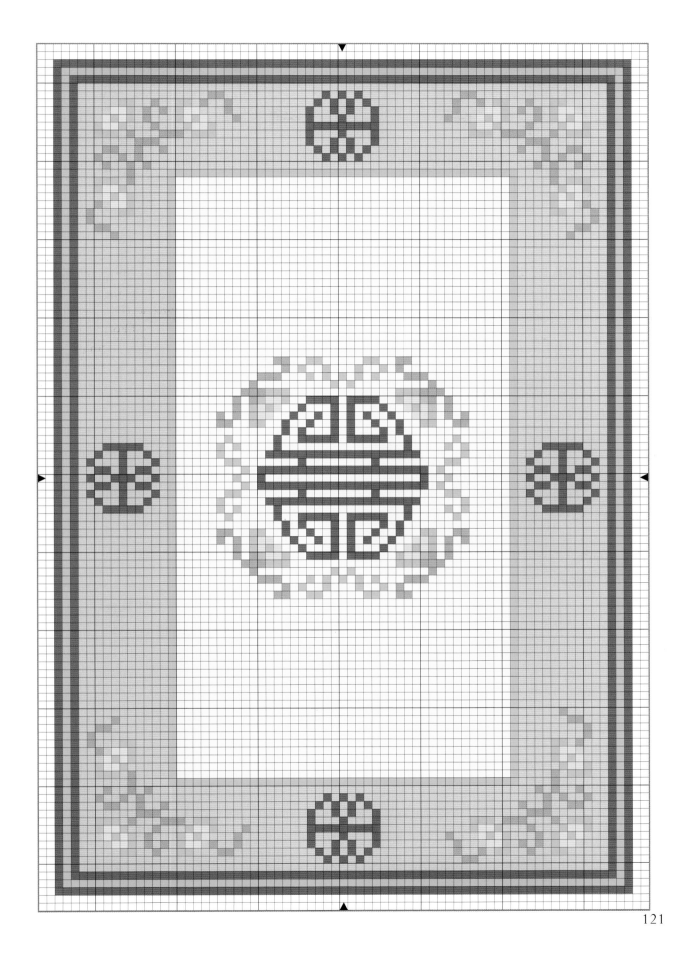

121

## Working method

**1**  It is advisable to first read the instructions for finishing the edges of the carpet, see Chapter 9.

**2**  Mount the canvas into a small embroidery frame and mark the vertical and horizontal centres with tacking stitches. These can be removed once a few embroidery stitches have been worked.

**3**  Referring to the chart on page 121, work from the centre. Each square on the chart represents one stitch over one thread of the canvas. Using two strands of stranded cotton, tent stitch throughout.

**4**  Remember not to work the third row in from the edge as this is used to turn the hem.

**5**  Work the motifs first and then fill in the surrounding background area.

**6**  When the embroidery is complete remove from the frame.

**7**  If the carpet has distorted, now is the time to block it back into shape (see Chapter 10).

**8**  Finally, trim the surplus canvas to six threads and complete the edges as described in Chapter 9.

# Chinese Cushion

This cushion uses the central motif of the carpet piece (pages 120–122), but the design would be equally suited to any square item.

## Working method

**1**   Mount the fabric into a small embroidery frame or card mount and mark the vertical and horizontal centres with tacking stitches. These tacking stitches can be removed once a few embroidery stitches have been worked.

**2**   Refer to the chart on page 121 and, using just the centre motif on the chart, begin working from the centre. Each square on the chart represents one stitch over one thread of the linen. Use one strand of stranded cotton and tent stitch throughout.

**3**   If using a coloured linen, the background need not be worked.

**4**   When the embroidery is complete remove from the frame.

**5**   Make up the cushion as directed in Chapter 9.

## Size

1¼in (32mm) square, or as desired

## Materials

Evenweave linen, 32 or 35 count: 4in (100mm) square

Lightweight fabric for back of cushion: 4in (100mm) square

Stranded cotton embroidery thread as listed in key: approx. 1yd (1m) each

Tacking cotton

Small rectangular embroidery frame or card mount

Tapestry needles: No. 26 or 28

Small amount of wadding or small plastic beads for filling

| | | DMC | Anchor | Madeira |
|---|---|---|---|---|
| | Rust | 356 | 1013 | 0402 |
| | Dark peach | 352 | 9 | 0303 |
| | Light peach | 353 | 868 | 0304 |
| | Olive green | 734 | 280 | 1610 |

# Lotus Cushion

The lotus is a favourite flower in Chinese art, and the delicate colours and shapes are ideally suited to embroidery designs.

The lotus flower represents creative power and purity amid adverse surroundings, and is a symbol of the seventh month, summer.

In China there are also many poems about the lotus, often describing how they come out of the dirty mud under the water and yet retain their pureness, freshness and beauty.

### Size

1½in (38mm) square

### Materials

Evenweave linen, 32 count: 4in (100mm) square

Lightweight fabric for back of cushion: 4in (100mm) square

Stranded cotton embroidery thread as listed in key: approx. 1yd (1m) each

Tacking cotton

Small rectangular embroidery frame or card mount

Tapestry needles: No. 26 or 28

Small amount of wadding or small plastic beads for filling

| | | DMC | Anchor | Madeira |
|---|---|---|---|---|
| | Dark green | 904 | 258 | 1413 |
| | Light green | 906 | 256 | 1410 |
| | Brown | 612 | 888 | 2108 |
| | Rust | 356 | 1013 | 0402 |
| | Dark peach | 352 | 9 | 0303 |
| | Light peach | 353 | 868 | 0304 |
| | Light flesh | 951 | 880 | 2308 |

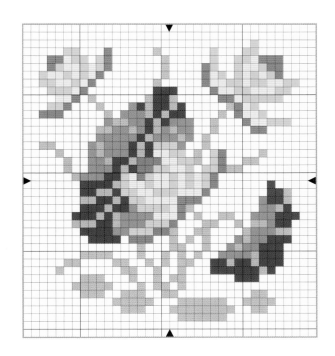

## Working method

**1**  Mount the fabric into a small embroidery frame or card mount and mark the vertical and horizontal centres with tacking stitches. These tacking stitches can be removed once a few embroidery stitches have been worked.

**2**  Refer to the chart and begin working from the centre. Each square on the chart represents one stitch over one thread of the linen. Use one strand of stranded cotton and tent stitch throughout.

**3**  If using a coloured linen, the background need not be worked.

**4**  When the embroidery is complete remove from the frame.

**5**  Make up the cushion as directed in Chapter 9.

# Peony Cushion

This peony cushion is a companion to the lotus cushion, and again uses the popular soft shades widely used in these tasteful Chinese designs.

The peony is known in China as the queen of flowers, or the flowers of riches, symbolizing wealth and distinction; paintings of peonies are often hung in the home for good luck. It is also one of the flowers of the four seasons and corresponds to late spring/early summer.

### Size

1½in (38mm) square

### Materials

Evenweave linen, 32 count: 4in (100mm) square

Lightweight fabric for back of cushion: 4in (100mm) square

Stranded cotton embroidery thread as listed in key: approx. 1yd (1m) each

Tacking cotton

Small rectangular embroidery frame or card mount

Tapestry needles: No. 26 or 28

Small amount of wadding or small plastic beads for filling

|  |  | DMC | Anchor | Madeira |
|---|---|---|---|---|
|  | Dark green | 904 | 258 | 1413 |
|  | Light green | 906 | 256 | 1410 |
|  | Dark pink | 892 | 28 | 0412 |
|  | Dark peach | 352 | 9 | 0303 |
|  | Light peach | 353 | 868 | 0304 |
|  | Light flesh | 951 | 880 | 2308 |
|  | Olive green | 732 | 281 | 1613 |

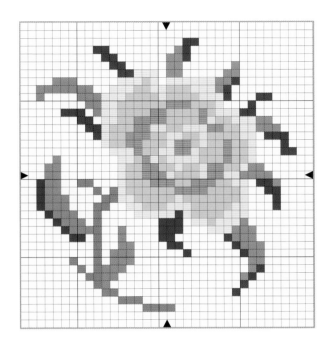

## Working method

**1**  Mount the fabric into a small embroidery frame or card mount and mark the vertical and horizontal centres with tacking stitches. These tacking stitches can be removed once a few embroidery stitches have been worked.

**2**  Refer to the chart and begin working from the centre. Each square on the chart represents one stitch over one thread of the linen. Use one strand of stranded cotton and tent stitch throughout.

**3**  If using a coloured linen, the background need not be worked.

**4**  When the embroidery is complete remove from the frame.

**5**  Make up the cushion as directed in Chapter 9.

# Pagoda Hanging

Pagodas with a setting of trees and grassy mounds are popular subjects. This project has been worked on coloured linen, although plain linen can be painted with dye. Instructions for this process are in Chapter 10.

### Size

3½ x 2⅛in (90 x 54mm)

### Materials

Evenweave linen, 32 count: 6 x 5in (150 x 126mm)

Evenweave fabric for hanging loops, 32 count: 6 x 1in (150 x 25mm)

Lightweight fabric to line the hanging: 6 x 5in (150 x 126mm)

Stranded cotton embroidery thread as listed in key: approx. 1yd (1m) each. 1 skein for background colour if used

Tacking cotton

Small rectangular embroidery frame

Tapestry needles: No. 26 or 28

|  |  | DMC | Anchor | Madeira |
|---|---|---|---|---|
|  | Dark green | 319 | 683 | 1313 |
|  | Mid green | 904 | 258 | 1413 |
|  | Light green | 906 | 256 | 1410 |
|  | Brown | 612 | 888 | 2108 |
|  | Rust | 356 | 1013 | 0402 |
|  | Dark peach | 352 | 9 | 0303 |
|  | Light peach | 353 | 868 | 0304 |
|  | Light flesh | 951 | 880 | 2308 |

## Working method

**1**   Mount the fabric into a small embroidery frame and mark the vertical and horizontal centres with tacking stitches. These stitches can be removed once a few embroidery stitches have been worked.

**2**   Refer to the chart on page 129 and work from the centre. Each square on the chart represents one stitch over one thread of the linen. Use one strand of stranded cotton and tent stitch throughout.

**3**   When the embroidery is complete remove from the frame.

**4**   Make up as directed in Chapter 9.

# Elephant Cushion

The elephant is considered a lucky motif and is widely used on Indian textiles, particularly those made for export or the tourist trade.

## Size

1½in (38mm) square

## Materials

Evenweave linen, 35 count: 4in (100mm) square

Lightweight fabric for the cushion back: 4in (100mm) square

Stranded cotton embroidery thread as listed in key; approx. 1yd (1m) each

Tacking cotton

Small rectangular embroidery frame or card mount

Tapestry needles: No. 26 or 28

Small amount of wadding or small plastic beads for filling

## Working method

**1** Mount the fabric into a small embroidery frame and mark the vertical and horizontal centres with tacking stitches. These stitches can be removed once a few embroidery stitches have been worked.

**2** Refer to the chart and begin working from the centre. Each square on the chart represents one

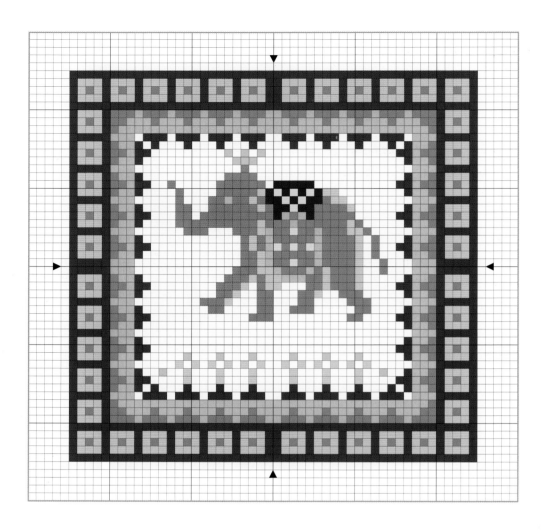

| | | DMC | Anchor | Madeira |
|---|---|---|---|---|
| | Light beige | 738 | 942 | 2013 |
| | Mid beige | 437 | 362 | 2012 |
| | Dark beige | 435 | 1046 | 2010 |
| | Brown | 801 | 359 | 2007 |
| | Cream (optional background) | 712 | 926 | 2101 |
| | Olive green | 732 | 281 | 1613 |
| | Dark green | 319 | 683 | 1313 |
| | Orange | 741 | 314 | 0201 |

stitch over one thread of the linen. Use one strand of stranded cotton and tent stitch throughout.

**3** When the embroidery is complete remove from the frame.

**4** Make up as directed in Chapter 9.

# Elephant Hanging

Featuring an elephant and a decorative mosaic tiled effect around the border, this little hanging shows a popular design format.

## Working method

The linen can be dyed if desired. Instructions for this can be found in Chapter 10.

**1**  Mount the fabric into a small embroidery frame and mark the vertical and horizontal centres with tacking stitches, which can be removed once a few embroidery stitches have been worked.

## Size

2⅜ x 2¹⁄₁₆in (60 x 52mm)

## Materials

Evenweave linen, 32 count: 5in (126mm) square, and a strip 5 x 1in (126 x 25mm) for hangers

Lightweight fabric to line the back if desired: 5in (126mm) square

Stranded cotton embroidery thread as listed in key: approx. 1yd (1m) each. 5yd (5m) for background colour, if used

Tacking cotton

Small rectangular embroidery frame

Tapestry needles: No. 26 or 28

**2**  Refer to the chart on page 134 and begin near the centre. Each square on the chart represents one stitch over one thread of the linen. Use one strand of stranded cotton and tent stitch throughout.

**3**  When the embroidery is complete remove from the frame and make up according to the instructions given in Chapter 9.

| | | DMC | Anchor | Madeira |
|---|---|---|---|---|
| | Beige | 738 | 942 | 2013 |
| | Dark beige | 437 | 362 | 2012 |
| | Tan | 435 | 1046 | 2010 |
| | Brown | 801 | 359 | 2007 |
| | Cream (background) | 712 | 926 | 2101 |
| | Olive | 732 | 281 | 1613 |
| | Dark green | 319 | 683 | 1313 |
| | Orange | 741 | 314 | 0201 |

# Red Cushion

This project is based on an Indian cover in a private collection, featuring stylized elephants and birds within decorative borders.

## Size

1½in (38mm) square

## Materials

Evenweave linen, 35 count: 4in (100mm) square

Lightweight fabric for the back of the cushion: 4in (100mm) square

Stranded cotton embroidery thread as listed in key: approx. 1yd (1m) each

Tacking cotton

Small rectangular embroidery frame or card mount

Tapestry needles: No. 26 or 28

Small amount of wadding or small plastic beads for filling

## Working method

**1**   Mount the fabric into a small embroidery frame or card mount and mark the vertical and horizontal centres with tacking stitches. These can be removed once a few embroidery stitches have been worked.

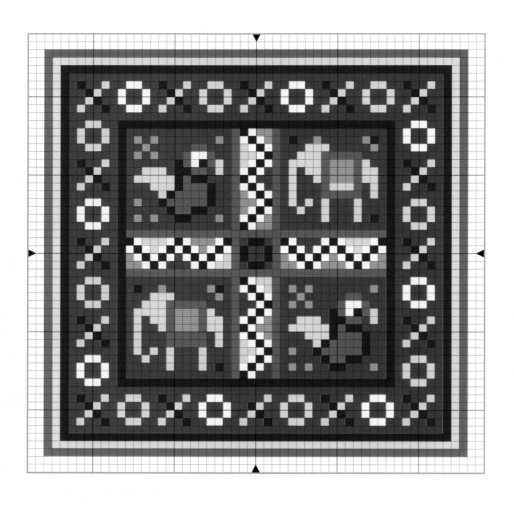

| | | DMC | Anchor | Madeira |
|---|---|---|---|---|
| | Red | 321 | 47 | 0510 |
| | Dark green | 319 | 683 | 1313 |
| | Yellow | 725 | 305 | 0106 |
| | Blue | 798 | 137 | 0911 |
| | White | Blanc | White | White |
| | Bright pink | 892 | 28 | 0412 |

**2** Refer to the chart above and work from the centre. Each square on the chart represents one stitch over one thread of the linen. Use one strand of stranded cotton and tent stitch throughout.

**3** When the embroidery is complete remove from the frame and make up and fill the cushion as described in Chapter 9.

# Toran Hanging

A Toran is a brightly coloured decorative hanging placed above a door or opening to encourage good luck. The lower edges are usually hung with tassels made from strips of rag. They are often embroidered with a variety of stitches enclosing shisha mirrors.

## Size

1⅜ x 3in (35 x 75mm)

## Materials

Evenweave linen, 35 count: 5in (126mm) square

Lightweight fabric to line the back: 5in (126mm) square

Stranded cotton embroidery thread as listed in key: approx. 1yd (1m) each

Tacking cotton

Small rectangular embroidery frame

Tapestry needles: No. 26 or 28

## Working method

**1** Mount the fabric into a small embroidery frame and mark the vertical and horizontal centres with tacking stitches. These stitches can be removed once a few embroidery stitches have been worked.

**2** Refer to the chart on page 138, and work from the centre. Each square on the chart represents one stitch over one thread of the linen. Use one strand of stranded cotton and tent stitch throughout.

**3** When the embroidery is complete remove from the frame and make up according to the instructions given in Chapter 9.

|  | DMC | Anchor | Madeira |
|---|---|---|---|
| Red | 321 | 47 | 0510 |
| Dark green | 319 | 683 | 1313 |
| Yellow | 725 | 305 | 0106 |
| Blue | 798 | 137 | 0911 |
| White | Blanc | White | White |
| Bright pink | 892 | 28 | 0412 |
| Orange | 740 | 316 | 0202 |

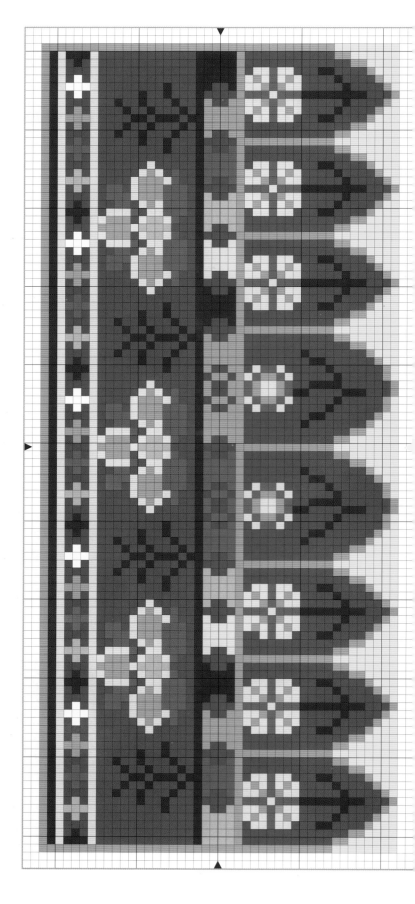

# Eastern European Patterns

These patterns are typical of the designs used for many household and costume items throughout Eastern Europe. They were used both individually, as motifs, and collectively to form more complex designs. They are particularly suited to cushions; any of the fabric counts suggested for cushions in this and the previous chapters can be used. The materials and working methods will be the same. The best colours to use for these designs are dark red, blue or green.

# 9
# Making Up and Finishing

The detailed instructions for making up and finishing items have been gathered together here to avoid constant repetition in the earlier chapters.

## Bedcovers

Bedcovers need to be made from lightweight, pliable fabrics, such as cotton, silk or linen, of at least 35 or 40 count. This will allow the cover to drape over the side of the bed. Some bedcovers will be the same size as the bed and will not need to hang over the sides. In this case other fabrics could be used, or the techniques of patchwork or quilting would be suitable. For patchwork and quilting designs see the previous volumes in this series, of Victorian and Georgian designs, which can also be used in a twentieth-century house.

For lining, use fine Habutai silk; it is not only very lightweight, but will take a dye beautifully and can be coloured to match the bedcover fabric.

### Making up a bedcover

**1** Remove from the embroidery frame and trim the outside edge turnings to about ¼in (6mm).

**2** Cut the lining to the same size.

**3** Fold under the outside edge turning of both the cover and the lining to be the same size.

**4** Place the cover and lining wrong sides together, see Fig 1.1 (page 141).

**5** Stitch the edges together with small hemming stitches using a sewing thread to match.

**6** To make the edge stay flat, work a row of running stitches through all the layers of the hems in a colour to match one of the embroidery threads.

### To make a bolster or pillow

**1** Cut two pieces of fine cotton or silk to the same size, either half or the full width of the bed.

**2** Turn the two long edges and one short end under, as for the bedcover.

**3** Stitch the three sides together.

**4** Fill the bolster or pillow with a small amount of wadding and sew up the remaining side.

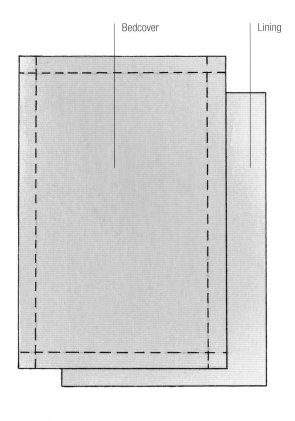

Bedcover

Lining

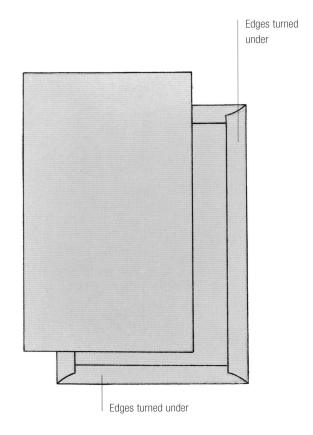

Edges turned under

Edges turned under

**Fig 1.1  Making up a bedcover**

# Carpets

The method of finishing carpets depends on the shape of the carpet and needs to be thought about when working the embroidery.

## Rectangular carpets

**1**   Initially, do not work the third row in from the edge of the carpet. This is done after the carpet has been blocked, so is part of the making up process.

**2**   When the carpet has been completed, except for the third row, remove from the frame and, if necessary, block back into shape as directed in Chapter 10.

**3**   Trim the edge turnings down to six threads of the canvas.

**4**  Cut away a small diagonal piece from the corners. Do not cut too much (see Fig 1.2, left).

**5**  Fold under the edges. The holes in the canvas will line up with those in the empty row between the embroidery stitches.

**6**  Work the remaining row through both layers (see Fig 1.2).

**7**  Finally, trim the excess canvas away close to the final stitching.

## Round carpets

**1**  Work all the rows and complete the embroidery for the carpet.

**2**  Trim the canvas from around the edge to about ¼in (6mm).

**3**  Fold under the edge turnings. The canvas will flatten when pressed with the fingers, especially where the grain falls on the bias or cross-grain.

**4**  Select a sewing cotton to match the colour in the carpet, or two colours if necessary.

**5**  With the sewing cotton, work a row of back stitch through the hem. Position the back stitches so they fall into the crevice between the embroidery stitches and disappear.

**6**  Alternatively, the edges can be secured into place by using a little PVA glue very sparingly.

## A semi-circular rug or carpet

**1**  Treat the straight edge as for a rectangular carpet, i.e. leave the third row un-worked initially.

**2**  Treat the rounded edges as for round carpets (see above).

**3**  Turn the curved edge first and then move on to the straight edge.

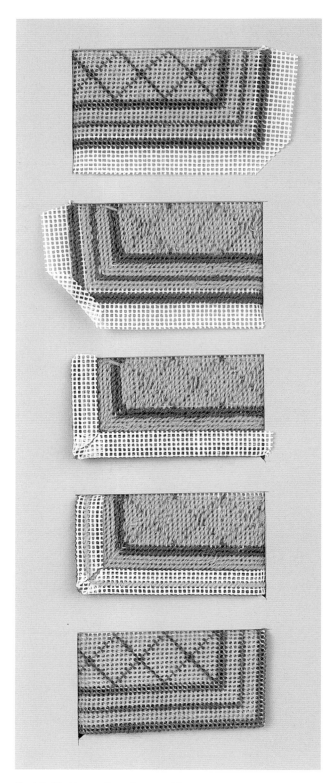

**Fig 1.2  Working rectangular carpet hems**

# Curtains

Most curtains in average twentieth-century houses hang simply from a rail or a pelmet. Instructions are given here for making this style.

If you require more elaborate hangings, refer to the Victorian and Georgian volumes in this series (also published by GMC Publications). The use of these styles in the twentieth century was in imitation of the earlier centuries.

For miniature curtains, the largest piece of fabric for draping is usually about 3in (75mm) wide by the desired length, depending on whether the curtain is full length or just to the sill.

## Gathering and making up the curtain

A pleater can be used, in which case, follow the manufacturer's instructions. The disadvantage of the pleater is that the folds are very regular and tend to look artificial.

A more realistic look is achieved by gathering in the same manner as for traditional smocking:

**1**   Cut the fabric to size allowing ½in (12mm) for hems and edge turnings.

**2**   Turn the lower edge hem and stitch. PVA glue can be used very sparingly if preferred. If the curtain is to hang from rings, the top hem will need to be turned also.

**3**   Turn and stitch, or glue, the side edges.

**4**   On the wrong side, mark a grid of dots with a soluble fabric pen or dressmakers' carbon (see Fig 1.3, below).

**5**   Thread a needle with polyester sewing thread and fasten on securely with a double stitch to one edge. Pick up a little fabric at each dot, working along the horizontal rows.

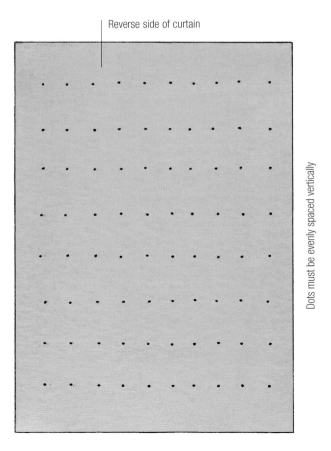

Reverse side of curtain

Dots must be evenly spaced vertically

**Fig 1.3  Placing of dots for gathering**

143

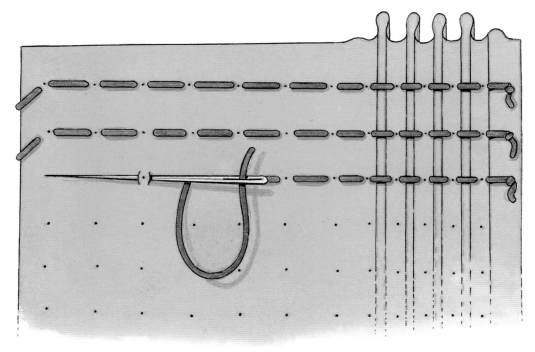

Reverse side of curtain

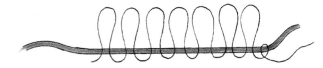

**Fig 1.4 Gathering the curtains**

End view after gathering

**6** Do not fasten off but leave a thread at the end of each row (see Fig 1.4, above).

**7** Complete all rows before gathering up.

**8** Draw up each gathering thread tightly and fasten off. Stroke a needle down the folds to smooth them.

**9** Either hold the pleated fabric in the steam of a kettle, using tongs to protect your fingers, or lightly press with a steam iron.

**10** Leave the curtain gathered up for as long as possible, certainly until completely dry.

**11** Gently unfasten the ends of the gathering threads and withdraw the thread.

**12** Either stitch small rings along the upper edge or make a pelmet as directed.

## Making pelmets

Four basic pelmet shapes are given in the patterns in Fig 1.5 (page 145).

**1** Copy the desired pattern on to card. Mounting card sold in art shops is suitable for this. The length of the pelmet can be adjusted in the centre.

**2** Cut out the shape around the outside edges with a craft knife and score along the inside lines.

**3** To cover the card, cut the fabric at least ½in (12mm) larger than the pelmet (Fig 1.6, page 146).

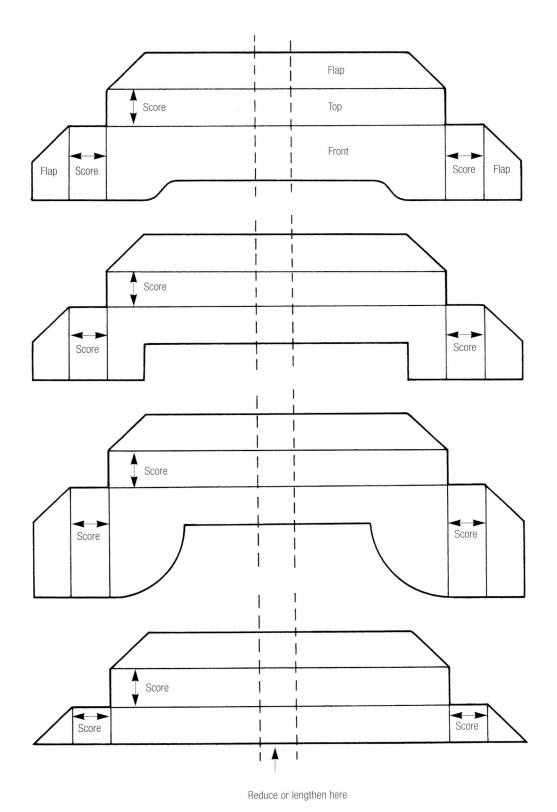

Reduce or lengthen here

**Fig 1.5  Patterns for pelmets**

**4** Apply a bonding agent, such as Bond-a-web, to the reverse of the fabric.

**5** Lay a sheet of non-stick baking paper on the work surface and use an iron to bond the fabric to the front of the card.

**6** Fold the turnings to the reverse of the card pelmet. Snip into corners where necessary to lay flat (see Fig 1.6, below).

**7** Add any braid or trimmings at this stage.

**8** Fold back all the top and side flaps along the scored lines.

**9** Check the length of the curtains and glue into place inside the pelmet.

**10** Use the turned-back flaps to glue into place at the window.

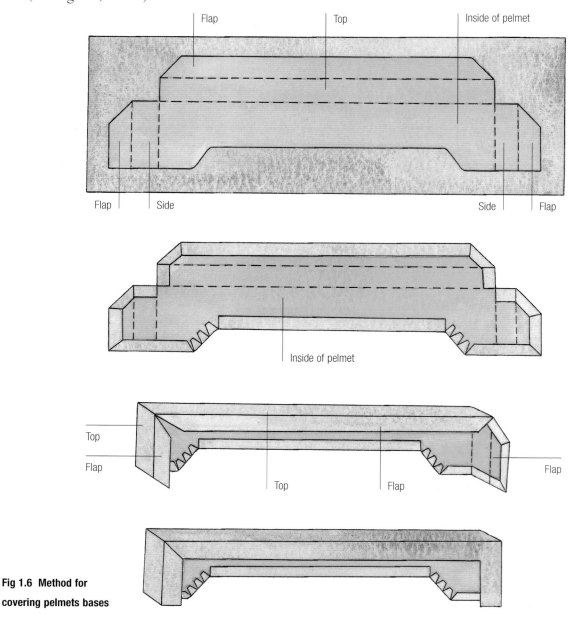

**Fig 1.6 Method for covering pelmets bases**

# Cushions

Most full-size cushions range from 15–20in (380–510mm) in size, and can be a variety of shapes. These making up instructions apply to all shapes and sizes. However, on curved shapes you may have to snip into turnings to reduce bulk.

For a firm cushion use wadding, but be sure not to over-stuff. For a 'lived-in' look, use small plastic or glass beads and fill the cushion to about two thirds. The cushion can then be placed and prodded with your finger to appear as if it has been used.

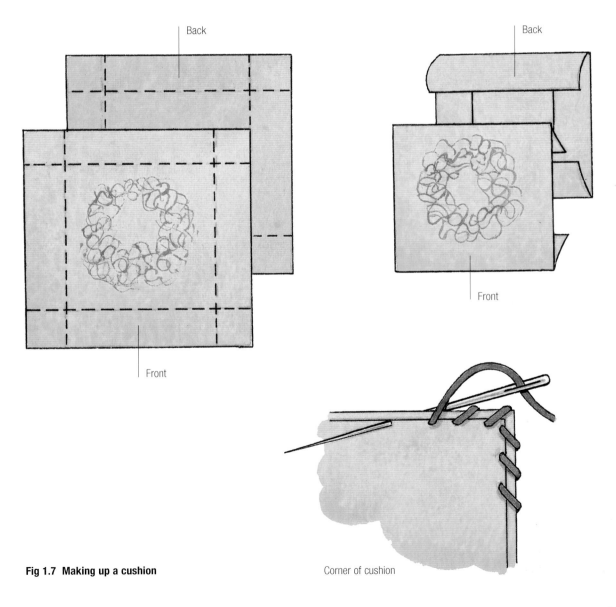

**Fig 1.7  Making up a cushion**

Corner of cushion

## Making up cushions

**1** Trim the seam allowances on the front and back to about ¼in (6mm) (see Fig 1.7, page 147).

**2** Fold under the edge turnings and stitch the front and back of the cushion together, leaving one side of it open.

**3** Fill the cushion as suggested on page 147 and stitch the opening closed.

**4** Complete the edging in one of the ways suggested in Fig 1.8 (below): a simple oversewn edge, a couched edge or a loop at each corner which is trimmed to simulate a tassel.

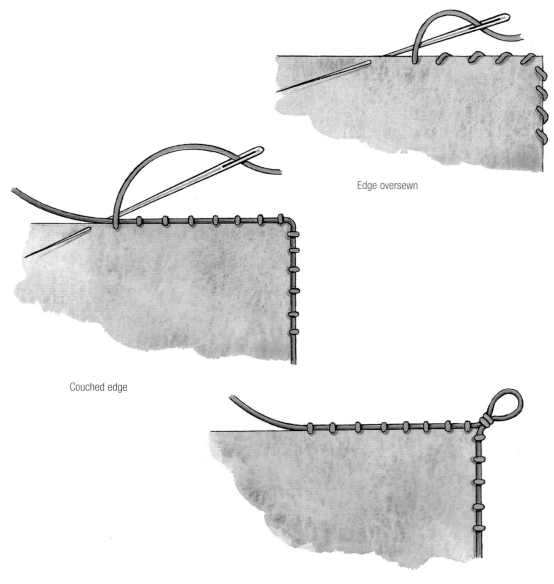

Edge oversewn

Couched edge

Loop left at corner for 'tassel'

**Fig 1.8 Edgings for cushions**

# Mounting and framing pictures and samplers

Miniature picture frame moulding comes in many styles, sizes and with or without a rebate.

The making of a frame is the same whether a rebate is used or not, but the method of mounting the fabric varies.

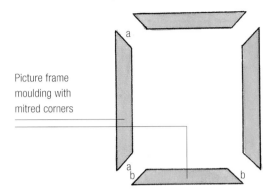

Picture frame moulding with mitred corners

## Making the frame

**1** Cut and mitre the moulding to fit the picture or sampler (see Fig 1.9). Remember that the required measurements, a-a and b-b, are the inside measurement of the mitred frame pieces and the finished size of the embroidered area.

**2** Carefully glue the corners of the frame, making sure that the corners are squared up.

**3** Stain and varnish or paint as required.

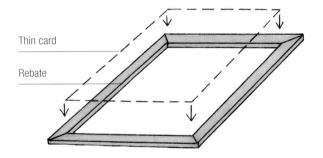

Thin card

Rebate

## Mounting the embroidery using a rebated frame

**1** Cut a piece of mounting card to fit exactly inside the rebate of the frame (see Fig 1.9).

**2** Cover the front of the card with a thin layer of PVA glue. Drag a piece of card over the surface to remove any excess.

**3** Place the embroidery in position on the tacky card; gently press down. Use the prepared frame to check that the position is correct and square.

**4** Leave to dry completely.

**5** Trim away the excess fabric and push the picture or sampler into the back of the frame. Secure with masking tape or cover the back with paper.

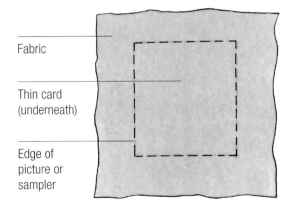

Fabric

Thin card (underneath)

Edge of picture or sampler

**Fig 1.9  Mounting using a rebated picture frame**

## Mounting using a flat-backed moulding

**1**   Cut a piece of mounting card 4in (100mm) square, or larger than the embroidered area.

**2**   Cover with a layer of PVA glue (see step 2 of 'Mounting the embroidery using a rebated frame'.

**3**   Place the embroidery on the tacky surface and lay the prepared frame over to ensure the position is correct (see Fig 2.0, below). Adjust if necessary.

**4**   When positioned, press down gently on to the tacky surface and leave to dry completely.

**5**   Using PVA glue very sparingly, secure the frame into position and leave to dry.

**6**   Finally, with a craft knife, cut away the surplus card and fabric in one operation.

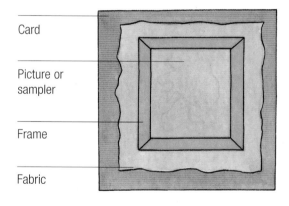

Card

Picture or sampler

Frame

Fabric

**Fig 2.0  Mounting using a flat-backed moulding**

# Making up screens

### Fire screens

**1**   Make a frame and mount the embroidery as described for a frame with or without a rebate.

**2**   Make two small 'feet' and glue to the lower edge of the screen as shown in Fig 2.1 (page 151).

### Three-fold screens

**1**   Stain and varnish or paint all of the stripwood.

**2**   Cut the stripwood to the sizes given for the various projects (see Fig 2.2, page 151). The Glasgow School and Jacobean screens have an extra horizontal strip to each panel.

**3**   Cover the front of each panel with a thin layer of PVA glue.

**4**   Allow to dry completely.

**5**   Place the embroidered panels into position on the dry glue, and secure the edges with a warm iron. Slightly stretch the fabric to ensure it lays flat. The dry PVA will heat seal where the iron touches.

**6**   Cut the narrow side pieces of stripwood and glue into place.

**7**   Cut the horizontal lengths carefully to fit exactly between the side pieces and glue into place (see Fig 2.2, page 151).

**Fig 2.1 Making up a fire screen**

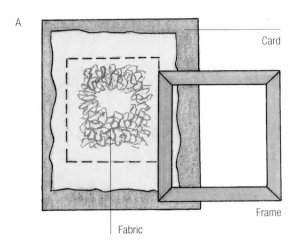

A

Card

Frame

Fabric

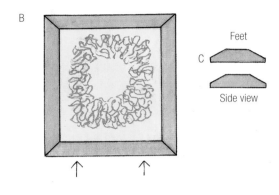

B

Feet

C

Side view

**Fig 2.2 Making up panels for a three-fold screen**

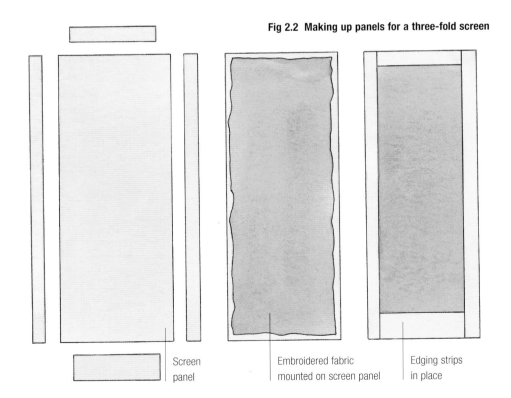

Screen
panel

Embroidered fabric
mounted on screen panel

Edging strips
in place

## Assembling the screen panels:

**1**  Place the backing – leather, Vilene or felt – onto the work surface. Do not cut to size or shape.

**2**  Spread PVA glue evenly and smoothly on the back of the second and third screen panels and lay side by side without a gap on the backing (see Fig 2.3a, below). Press gently into place and allow to dry completely. Make sure that no surplus glue rises between the panels.

**3**  Place the first screen panel face down on top of the second (see Fig 2.3b).

**4**  Spread glue sparingly over the backing beside the two original panels.

**5**  Fold the backing over the first panel, ensuring the hinge area is glued (see Fig 2.3b). Leave to dry.

**6**  When dry, open the screen to lay flat. If the hinge, or any of the backing, has not adhered completely, press the backing with a warm iron to seal (see Fig 2.3c).

**7**  With a craft knife, cut away the excess backing.

**8**  Finally, fold the screen (as shown in Fig 2.3d) and stand upright.

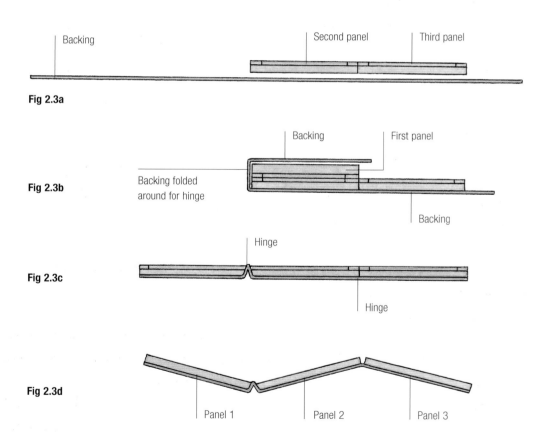

**Fig 2.3a**

**Fig 2.3b**  Backing folded around for hinge

**Fig 2.3c**

**Fig 2.3d**

**Fig 2.3  Assembling the panels for the three-fold screen**

# Making up wall hangings

Wall hangings can be hung with loops along the upper edge to be suspended from a pole, or can be mounted within panelling as permanent fixtures.

## To mount wall hangings within panelling

**1** Make the frame for the panelling with miniature picture frame mouldings or dado rail in the same manner as a picture frame (see page 149).
**2** Mount the embroidery as instructed for mounting pictures and samplers in a frame without a rebate (see page 150).
**3** Secure into position on the wall with glue or a grip wax.

## A free-hanging panel

**1** Trim the edges to ½in (12mm) for turnings.
**2** Fold under the upper and lower edges and press into place with an iron.
**3** Trim a little excess from the corners of the turnings.
**4** Fold under the side edges and press.
**5** Make the hanging loops. Cut a strip of the fabric used for the hanging about ¼in (20mm) wide and 6in (150mm) long.
**6** Fold lengthways a little under a third of the width and press (see Fig 2.4).
**7** Fold remaining side and secure with either stitches or a little PVA glue (see Fig 2.4).

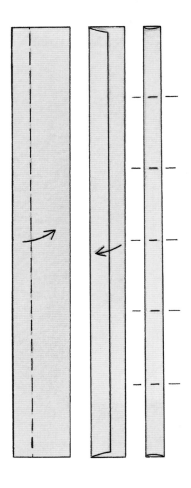

**Fig 2.4  Making the hanging loops for wall hangings**

**8** Cut into the required number of pieces. Fold in half and stitch into position on the reverse of the top edge of the hanging.
**9** Cover the back with a lightweight fabric lining with the edges turned and stitch into position.

# 10
## General Hints and Tips

## Measurements

It is important to repeat that the metric and imperial measurements given are alternatives and not intended to be exact conversions. Please only use one or the other, not a combination of both.

## Suitable fabrics

Canvas has been used for projects for carpets and rugs. Canvas is available in various counts; the number of threads to the inch. Single-thread canvas, also known as mono canvas, has been used for the projects.

Coin net is a name for a cotton canvas with a count of 24 threads, but other canvases can be purchased in the same count.

Interlock canvas is very good as it is more pliable than some of the stiffer canvases – it has a twisted weave, as it was originally used to be cut to shape and the weave stops the canvas fraying.

Evenweave linens are suitable for miniature work as they can be purchased in many fine counts; 32, 35 and 40 being readily available. Evenweave cotton fabrics are not so good as the woven thread is very fluffy compared to linen.

Silk gauze is ideal, but rather more difficult to purchase and much more expensive. It also necessitates the filling-in of the background which is not always the case with linen.

### Fabrics for linings

It is essential that only lightweight fabrics are used to line a miniature item. Habutai silk is ideal; it is fine and can be coloured very easily. Alternatively, cotton lawn works well and takes a dye. Try to avoid synthetics as they do not fold well or press flat.

### Wadding for filling cushions

Quilting wadding, teased into small pieces, and synthetic toy filling, work well. Small plastic or glass beads can be used for filling cushions (see 'Making up cushions', pages 147–148).

# Using embroidery frames

The use of an embroidery frame will help to stop the embroidered piece from distorting. Most of the projects in this volume only require a small frame. However, if you wish to work several pieces in the same frame, a slate frame might be required.

## The slate frame

This is a rectangular frame with two sides with circular notches, into which two rounded sides with webbing are fixed with wing nuts (Fig 3.1).

**1**  Dismantle the frame and stitch the fabric to the two lengths of webbing.

**2**  Reassemble the frame and turn the rounded sides to tension the fabric; tighten the wing nuts.

**3**  Using a strong thread, tension the straight sides by lacing with the threads as shown.

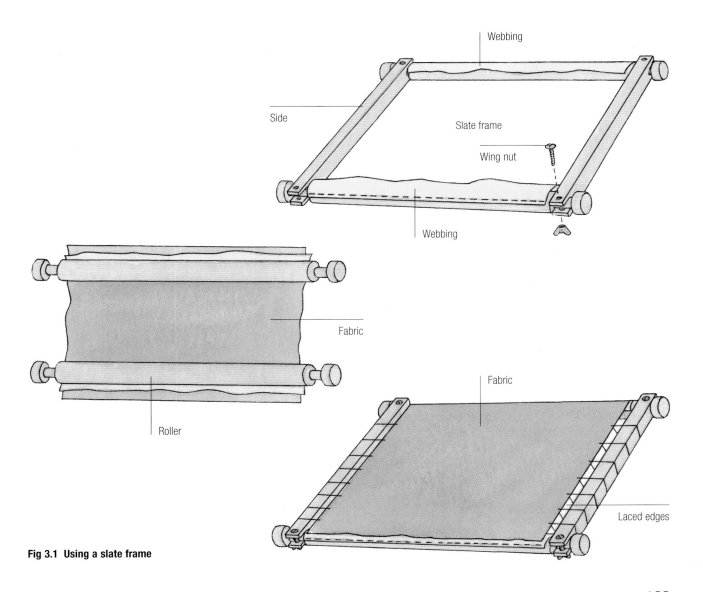

**Fig 3.1  Using a slate frame**

### Stretcher frames

It is possible to purchase from needlework shops a set of miniature stretcher frames which push together at the corners by means of a tongue-and-groove joint. The sides are simply pushed together and a variety of sizes can be achieved. The fabric is fitted into the frame with drawing pins (thumb tacks) (see Fig 3.2, below).

# Card mounts

For very small items a card mount can be made.

**1**   Cut a piece of card, mounting card is ideal, 4in (100mm) square.

**2**   Remove a 2in (50mm) square from the centre.

**3**   On the reverse side, using PVA wood glue, spread a line of glue around the central window opening. Allow to dry completely. See Fig. 3.3.

**4**   Place the fabric over the opening and secure into place by pressing with a hot iron.

**5**   The fabric will thus be in place without any glue marking it. If it loosens during working, simply apply the iron again.

**6**   On completion, the fabric will peel off.

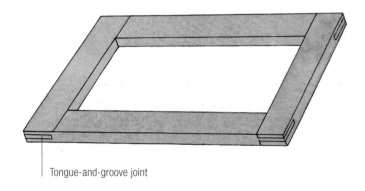

Tongue-and-groove joint

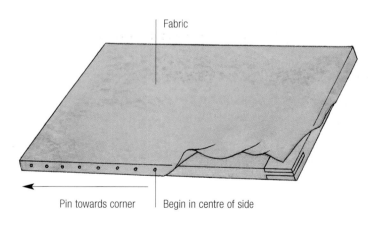

Fabric

Pin towards corner | Begin in centre of side

**Fig 3.2  Using a stretcher frame**

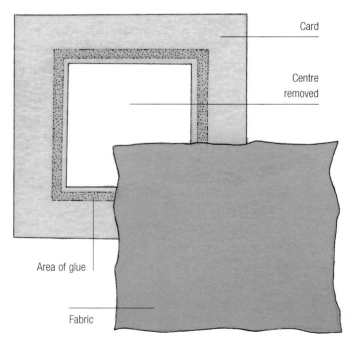

Card

Centre removed

Area of glue

Fabric

**Fig 3.3  Making a card mount for small items**

# Beginning to stitch on canvas or evenweave

**1**   To begin, make a knot in the end of the embroidery thread.

**2**   Pass the needle through the fabric from the right side a little way away from the starting point. Allow the knot to sit on the right side of the fabric. There will be a length of thread on the wrong side between the knot and the starting point.

**3**   Begin the embroidery.

**4**   When some of the stitches have worked over the length of thread on the wrong side, the knot can be cut off.

**5**   Eventually, all ends will be covered.

# Colouring fabrics

There are many types of fabric dyes and paints on the market and the manufacturers instructions for fixing the colour should be followed. This usually means applying heat with an iron. However, if the item is not going to be laundered, any colouring medium can be used.

It is possible to colour the evenweave linen if desired. However, as the fabric contains a high level of natural oils, more than one application may be necessary to achieve the shade required.

**1**   It is best to mount the fabric into a simple frame to hold it rigid.

**2**   The colouring, dye or paint, can then be applied with a paint brush.

**3**   Leave the fabric to dry naturally in a horizontal position: if you tilt it, the colour will not dry evenly.

**4**   Press with an iron when dry.

## Fabric transfer paints

These paints are designed to be used initially on paper and then ironed off onto fabric. They are intended for synthetic fabrics but will work on natural fibres giving a slightly softer colour. There are two things that need to be considered:

**1**   The colours seen on the paper are not the same as when ironed off. A test strip should be made first using the intended fabric, allowing the colours to be adjusted.

**2**   The design is reversed when ironed off. This may not matter unless there is lettering.

The designs for curtains can be achieved with these paints, producing very effective results.

# Blocking distorted embroidery

Counted thread embroidery may distort due to the tension of the stitches. This can be rectified by blocking the piece.

**1**   First, check that all the embroidery threads are colour-fast. This may be the case if you have substituted something other than stranded cotton.

**2**   Take a piece of pin board, or other board soft enough the take pins or drawing pins. The board needs to be larger than the embroidery including the turnings.

**3**   Draw a rectangle on a sheet of paper, larger than embroidery, to act as a guide to squaring up. Lay the paper on the board.

**4**   Cover the board and paper with plastic film to prevent the board staining the work.

**5**   Using the line as a guide, begin pinning the piece to be blocked; start in the centre of one side.

**6**   Slightly stretch the fabric and continue to pin towards a corner (see Fig 3.4, below). Returning to the centre, pin to the other corner.

**8**   Repeat with the opposite side ensuring that the grain of the fabric is straight across the centre.

**9**   When all four sides are stretched, leave to dry naturally.

**10** If the piece is badly distorted, the process may need to be repeated.

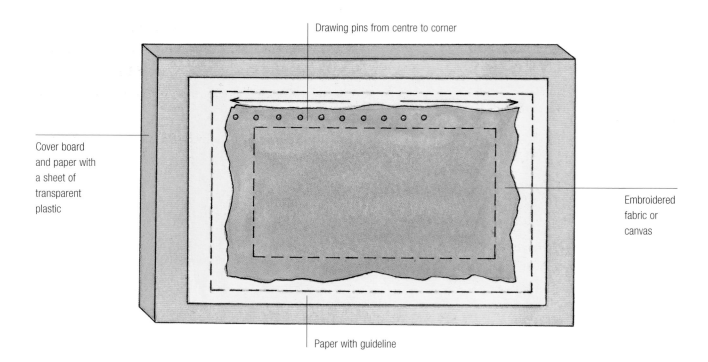

Drawing pins from centre to corner

Cover board and paper with a sheet of transparent plastic

Embroidered fabric or canvas

Paper with guideline

**Fig 3.4  Blocking a completed piece of canvaswork**

# 11
## Stitch Glossary

# Methods of fastening on

The old rule that 'thou shalt not start with a knot' derives from a time when most embroidered articles had to be laundered, and a knot would unravel in the washing process.

With miniatures, which are unlikely to need repeated washing, it is sometimes an advantage to begin with a small knot. However, the best method, once some stitching has been worked, is to secure the beginning of the thread into the back of the existing stitching.

## Backstitch

A stitch that makes a line.

Bring the needle up through from the back of the fabric and take it down again to give the length of stitch required. Bring the needle up through the fabric again, the length of a stitch away from the previous stitch (at 1). Take the needle back through the fabric, next to the previous stitch (2).

When complete, fasten off into the back of the stitches.

## Blanket or buttonhole stitch

This stitch can form an edging, a row of stitching, or be radiated to form a flower effect.

Bring the needle up through the fabric at 1, and take it down at 2, a little to one side of 1. Pick up a stitch (2 to 3) to give the desired length and

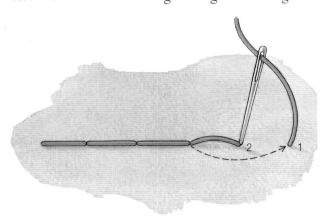

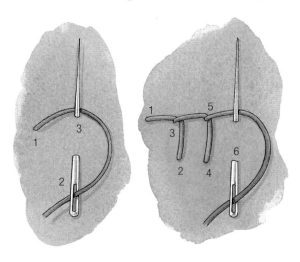

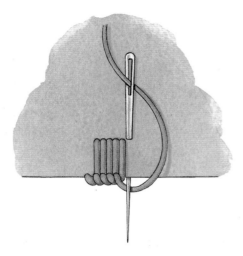

direction. Bring the needle back through, making sure the thread is behind the needle. Continue this way (4 to 5) keeping the thread behind the needle.

When complete, fasten off into the back of the stitches.

Buttonhole stitch is worked in the same way, but with the stitches very close together.

## Couching

This method is used to lay a thread on the surface of the fabric, which is stitched down with a second, finer thread.

Bring the thread to be laid through from the back of the fabric. In another needle, bring the sewing

thread through from the back, immediately beside the first thread (1), and take a stitch over the first thread. Continue to secure the first thread in this manner, at the same time moving the first thread, if necessary, to form the shape or line required.

Fasten the sewing thread off behind the stitching, then take the first thread through to the back and fasten it off.

## Cross stitch

The diagram shows the method for working a row of cross stitch by making the first half of each stitch all the way along the row and then working the second half on the way back along the row.

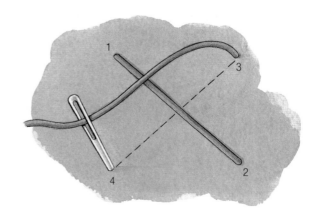

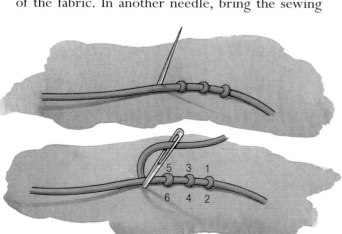

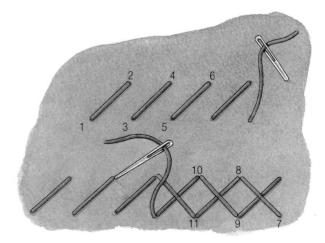

Individual crosses can be worked by making the two stitches immediately one after the other. Which method you choose will depend on the design.

Fasten off in the back of the stitching.

## Cushion stitch

Cushion stitch forms a square of diagonal stitches. Each alternate square has the stitches sloping in the opposite direction (see diagram below).

The first stitch is worked diagonally over one thread, the second over two, and the third over three. The fourth stitch is worked over two threads and the final stitch over one, thus forming a square.

To begin working the next square, bring the needle up at 11 as shown, and take it down at 12.

## Darning

This stitch is worked only on evenweave fabrics or canvas and produces a regular pattern. A tapestry needle must be used.

Fasten off into the back of the stitching.

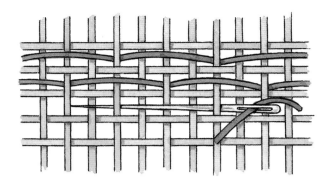

## Detached chain stitch

This stitch is useful for flowers and leaves. A short stitch produces a rounded shape while a longer stitch produces a narrower shape.

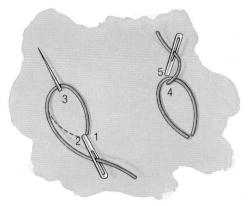

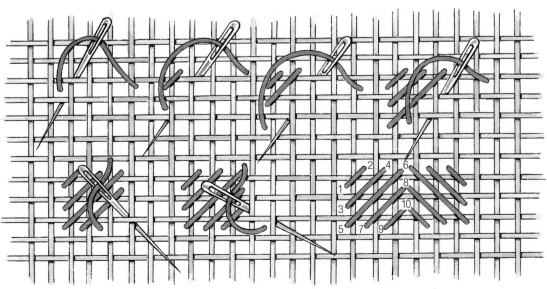

Bring the needle up through the back of the fabric (1), then take it down as close as possible to the same point (2). Bring the needle up again at 3, making a stitch of the length required, and looping the thread under the needle. Pull the thread through and take a small stitch over the loop to secure it (4).

When complete, fasten off in the back of the stitching.

## Feather stitch

Bring the needle through from the back of the fabric and make a stitch at an angle, forming a triangle, with the thread under the needle. Draw the thread through.

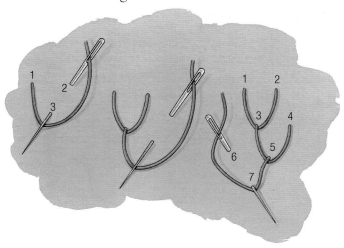

Continue taking stitches at an angle, first to one side, then to the other.

When the required number of stitches are completed, take a small stitch over the last loop to secure.

## French knot

This stitch can be used alone or clustered together.

Bring the needle through from the back of the fabric and wind the thread once around the needle. Take the point of the needle back through the fabric, very close to where the thread was brought through to the front. Draw the thread through to the back of the fabric. When complete, this will form a neat, compact knot.

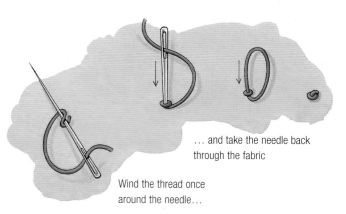

... and take the needle back
through the fabric

Wind the thread once
around the needle...

## Hemming

This stitch is used to secure a hem. Turn the edge of the fabric over as desired. Pick up a little of the fabric and the turned hem and draw the thread through, repeating until the entire hem is secure. Only a tiny stitch should show on the right side of the fabric, so it is an advantage to use a very fine needle.

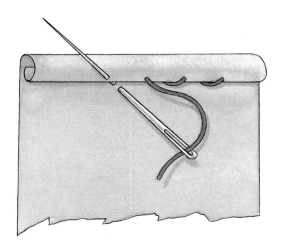

# Herringbone stitch

Herringbone stitch is generally used to give a decorative border, but can also be used as a filling stitch in some places.

Bring the needle through from the back of the fabric and make a diagonal stitch. Bring the needle back through a short space away horizontally. Make another diagonal stitch which crosses over the first. Continue until complete.

Fasten off into the back of the stitching.

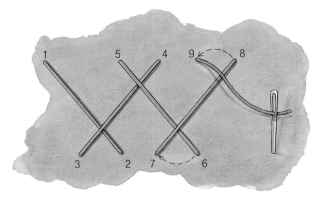

# Holbein stitch

A reversible double running stitch used on collars, cuffs and where both sides of the fabric would be seen.

# Running stitch

This stitch is basically the same as darning, but it is worked on a plain fabric and not counted. It can be used for outlining and in quilting.

The needle is simply taken in and out of the fabric to form the line or shape required.

If the stitch is used for quilting, a smaller stitch can be obtained by stab stitching. Take the needle through the fabrics and draw the thread through, then, in a second movement, bring the needle and thread back through the fabrics again. Work each stitch in two movements.

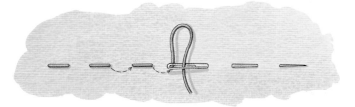

# Satin stitch

This stitch is used as a filling for small areas. Bring the needle through from the back of the fabric, on the outline of the shape. Take the needle back through the fabric on the opposite side of the shape. Continue to place stitches next to one another in this manner until the shape is filled. Fasten off into the back of the stitching.

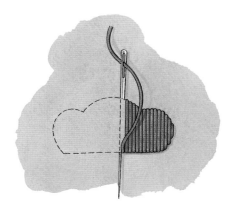

## Seeding stitches

Seeding is an effect created by short, straight stitches scattered at various angles. Traditionally, two stitches were used side by side, but for miniature work one is sufficient.

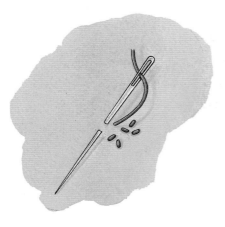

## Straight stitch

Straight stitch is the most basic and versatile embroidery stitch. It can be used for tiny leaves or flowers. It is simply a single stitch which can be of any length, and used side by side or set at an angle to radiate.

Bring the needle through from the back of the fabric and take it down again to make a stitch of the length required. Continue laying stitches in this way to give the effect that you require.

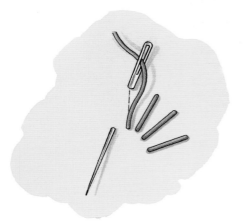

## Tent stitch

This stitch is used on an evenweave fabric or canvas. By using tent stitch, rather than half cross stitch, the stitches can be worked in any direction and will look exactly the same on the front. Tent stitch also prevents the thread from slipping behind the weave of the fabric and disappearing.

The top diagram shows the placing of the needle. The numbered diagram gives the sequence for different directions. Bring the needle up through the odd numbers and take the needle back down through the even numbers.

When rows are worked next to one another, the same holes are used as the previous row. Do not leave a thread of canvas empty in between.

Tent stitch can also slope from top left to bottom right.

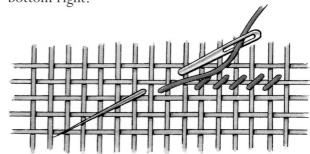

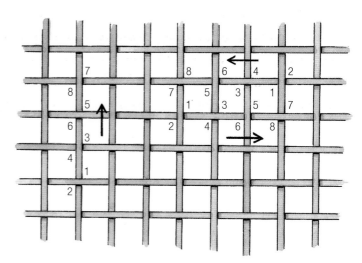

# About the Author

Pamela Warner's interest in embroidery began in the mid-1950s with her studies for a National Design Diploma (NDD) in fashion – which included embroidery – at Bromley College of Art in London.

After a career in banking and computing, followed by marriage and a family, Pamela rediscovered creative embroidery at an evening class. She went on to qualify, and by 1979 was teaching embroidery for Bromley Adult Education and the Inner London Education Authority (ILEA). During the early 1980s she was a tutor for City and Guilds embroidery classes at Bromley, and eventually took on full responsibility for the course.

Pamela discovered dolls' houses in 1989. She began with a ready-made house and a kit, but was soon frustrated with the small rooms. In order to learn the craft, she went on a Dolls' House Holiday, with Peter Alden, and was so impressed with the results that she keeps returning.

Her work as a professional embroiderer has been exhibited widely, and she has undertaken many commissions for ecclesiastic and secular pieces. She has also spent 15 years restoring and conserving embroideries for Westminster Abbey in London, and other churches.

Pamela has recently retired and keeps her interest going with contact with interested groups of miniaturists, the Embroiderers' Guild and the Miniature Needlework Society.

This is Pamela's sixth book, following *Embroidery: A History*, *Tudor Treasures to Embroider*, *Miniature Embroidery for the Victorian Dolls' House*, and subsequent volumes *Miniature Embroidery for the Georgian Dolls' House* and *Miniature Embroidery for the Tudor and Stuart Dolls' House*, as well as a series of booklets on the history of embroidery.

# Index

Page numbers in **bold** refer to illustrations.

# GMC Publications

## BOOKS

### Woodcarving

| | |
|---|---|
| Beginning Woodcarving | GMC Publications |
| Carving Architectural Detail in Wood: The Classical Tradition | Frederick Wilbur |
| Carving Birds & Beasts | GMC Publications |
| Carving the Human Figure: Studies in Wood and Stone | Dick Onians |
| Carving Nature: Wildlife Studies in Wood | Frank Fox-Wilson |
| Carving on Turning | Chris Pye |
| Celtic Carved Lovespoons: 30 Patterns | Sharon Littley & Clive Griffin |
| Decorative Woodcarving (New Edition) | Jeremy Williams |
| Elements of Woodcarving | Chris Pye |
| Essential Woodcarving Techniques | Dick Onians |
| Figure Carving in Wood: Human and Animal Forms | Sara Wilkinson |
| Lettercarving in Wood: A Practical Course | Chris Pye |
| Relief Carving in Wood: A Practical Introduction | Chris Pye |
| Woodcarving for Beginners | GMC Publications |
| Woodcarving Made Easy | Cynthia Rogers |
| Woodcarving Tools, Materials & Equipment (New Edition in 2 vols.) | Chris Pye |

### Woodturning

| | |
|---|---|
| Bowl Turning Techniques Masterclass | Tony Boase |
| Chris Child's Projects for Woodturners | Chris Child |
| Contemporary Turned Wood: New Perspectives in a Rich Tradition | Ray Leier, Jan Peters & Kevin Wallace |
| Decorating Turned Wood: The Maker's Eye | Liz & Michael O'Donnell |
| Green Woodwork | Mike Abbott |
| Intermediate Woodturning Projects | GMC Publications |
| Keith Rowley's Woodturning Projects | Keith Rowley |
| Making Screw Threads in Wood | Fred Holder |
| Segmented Turning: A Complete Guide | Ron Hampton |
| Turned Boxes: 50 Designs | Chris Stott |
| Turning Green Wood | Michael O'Donnell |
| Turning Pens and Pencils | Kip Christensen & Rex Burningham |
| Woodturning: Forms and Materials | John Hunnex |
| Woodturning: A Foundation Course (New Edition) | Keith Rowley |
| Woodturning: A Fresh Approach | Robert Chapman |
| Woodturning: An Individual Approach | Dave Regester |
| Woodturning: A Source Book of Shapes | John Hunnex |
| Woodturning Masterclass | Tony Boase |
| Woodturning Techniques | GMC Publications |

### Woodworking

| | |
|---|---|
| Beginning Picture Marquetry | Lawrence Threadgold |
| Celtic Carved Lovespoons: 30 Patterns | Sharon Littley & Clive Griffin |
| Celtic Woodcraft | Glenda Bennett |
| Complete Woodfinishing (Revised Edition) | Ian Hosker |
| David Charlesworth's Furniture-Making Techniques | David Charlesworth |
| David Charlesworth's Furniture-Making Techniques – Volume 2 | David Charlesworth |
| Furniture-Making Projects for the Wood Craftsman | GMC Publications |
| Furniture-Making Techniques for the Wood Craftsman | GMC Publications |
| Furniture Projects with the Router | Kevin Ley |
| Furniture Restoration (Practical Crafts) | Kevin Jan Bonner |
| Furniture Restoration: A Professional at Work | John Lloyd |
| Furniture Restoration and Repair for Beginners | Kevin Jan Bonner |
| Furniture Restoration Workshop | Kevin Jan Bonner |
| Green Woodwork | Mike Abbott |
| Intarsia: 30 Patterns for the Scrollsaw | John Everett |
| Kevin Ley's Furniture Projects | Kevin Ley |
| Making Chairs and Tables – Volume 2 | GMC Publications |
| Making Classic English Furniture | Paul Richardson |
| Making Heirloom Boxes | Peter Lloyd |
| Making Screw Threads in Wood | Fred Holder |
| Making Woodwork Aids and Devices | Robert Wearing |
| Mastering the Router | Ron Fox |
| Pine Furniture Projects for the Home | Dave Mackenzie |
| Router Magic: Jigs, Fixtures and Tricks to Unleash your Router's Full Potential | Bill Hylton |
| Router Projects for the Home | GMC Publications |
| Router Tips & Techniques | Robert Wearing |
| Routing: A Workshop Handbook | Anthony Bailey |
| Routing for Beginners | Anthony Bailey |
| Sharpening: The Complete Guide | Jim Kingshott |
| Space-Saving Furniture Projects | Dave Mackenzie |
| Stickmaking: A Complete Course | Andrew Jones & Clive George |
| Stickmaking Handbook | Andrew Jones & Clive George |
| Storage Projects for the Router | GMC Publications |
| Veneering: A Complete Course | Ian Hosker |
| Veneering Handbook | Ian Hosker |
| Woodworking Techniques and Projects | Anthony Bailey |
| Woodworking with the Router: Professional Router Techniques any Woodworker can Use | Bill Hylton & Fred Matlack |

### Upholstery

| | |
|---|---|
| Upholstery: A Complete Course (Revised Edition) | David James |
| Upholstery Restoration | David James |
| Upholstery Techniques & Projects | David James |
| Upholstery Tips and Hints | David James |

### Toymaking

| | |
|---|---|
| Scrollsaw Toy Projects | Ivor Carlyle |
| Scrollsaw Toys for All Ages | Ivor Carlyle |

# Dolls' Houses and Miniatures

# Crafts

# Gardening

Creating Contrast with Dark Plants    *Freya Martin*
Creating Small Habitats for Wildlife in your Garden    *Josie Briggs*
Exotics are Easy    *GMC Publications*
Gardening with Hebes    *Chris & Valerie Wheeler*
Gardening with Shrubs    *Eric Sawford*
Gardening with Wild Plants    *Julian Slatcher*
Growing Cacti and Other Succulents in the Conservatory
   and Indoors    *Shirley-Anne Bell*
Growing Cacti and Other Succulents in the Garden    *Shirley-Anne Bell*
Growing Successful Orchids in the Greenhouse
   and Conservatory    *Mark Isaac-Williams*
Hardy Palms and Palm-Like Plants    *Martyn Graham*
Hardy Perennials: A Beginner's Guide    *Eric Sawford*
Hedges: Creating Screens and Edges    *Averil Bedrich*
How to Attract Butterflies to your Garden    *John & Maureen Tampion*
Marginal Plants    *Bernard Sleeman*
Orchids are Easy: A Beginner's Guide to their Care and Cultivation    *Tom Gilland*
Plant Alert: A Garden Guide for Parents    *Catherine Collins*
Planting Plans for Your Garden    *Jenny Shukman*
Sink and Container Gardening Using Dwarf Hardy Plants    *Chris & Valerie Wheeler*
The Successful Conservatory and Growing Exotic Plants    *Joan Phelan*
Success with Cuttings    *Chris & Valerie Wheeler*
Success with Seeds    *Chris & Valerie Wheeler*
Tropical Garden Style with Hardy Plants    *Alan Hemsley*
Water Garden Projects: From Groundwork to Planting    *Roger Sweetinburgh*

## Photography

Close-Up on Insects    *Robert Thompson*
Digital Enhancement for Landscape Photographers
   *Arjan Hoogendam & Herb Parkin*
Double Vision    *Chris Weston & Nigel Hicks*
An Essential Guide to Bird Photography    *Steve Young*
Field Guide to Bird Photography    *Steve Young*
Field Guide to Landscape Photography    *Peter Watson*
How to Photograph Pets    *Nick Ridley*
In my Mind's Eye: Seeing in Black and White    *Charlie Waite*
Life in the Wild: A Photographer's Year    *Andy Rouse*

Light in the Landscape: A Photographer's Year    *Peter Watson*
*Outdoor Photography* Portfolio    *GMC Publications*
Photographers on Location with Charlie Waite    *Charlie Waite*
Photographing Fungi in the Field    *George McCarthy*
Photography for the Naturalist    *Mark Lucock*
Photojournalism: An Essential Guide    *David Herrod*
Professional Landscape and Environmental Photography:
   From 35mm to Large Format    *Mark Lucock*
Rangefinder    *Roger Hicks & Frances Schultz*
Underwater Photography    *Paul Kay*
Viewpoints from *Outdoor Photography*    *GMC Publications*
Where and How to Photograph Wildlife    *Peter Evans*
Wildlife Photography Workshops    *Steve & Ann Toon*

## Art Techniques

Oil Paintings from your Garden: A Guide for Beginners    *Rachel Shirley*

# VIDEOS

Drop-in and Pinstuffed Seats    *David James*
Stuffover Upholstery    *David James*
Elliptical Turning    *David Springett*
Woodturning Wizardry    *David Springett*
Turning Between Centres: The Basics    *Dennis White*
Turning Bowls    *Dennis White*
Boxes, Goblets and Screw Threads    *Dennis White*
Novelties and Projects    *Dennis White*
Classic Profiles    *Dennis White*
Twists and Advanced Turning    *Dennis White*
Sharpening the Professional Way    *Jim Kingshott*
Sharpening Turning & Carving Tools    *Jim Kingshott*
Bowl Turning    *John Jordan*
Hollow Turning    *John Jordan*
Woodturning: A Foundation Course    *Keith Rowley*
Carving a Figure: The Female Form    *Ray Gonzalez*
The Router: A Beginner's Guide    *Alan Goodsell*
The Scroll Saw: A Beginner's Guide    *John Burke*

# MAGAZINES

Woodturning ◆ Woodcarving ◆ Furniture & Cabinetmaking ◆ The Router
New Woodworking ◆ The Dolls' House Magazine ◆ Outdoor Photography
Black & White Photography ◆ Travel Photography ◆ Machine Knitting News
Knitting ◆ Guild of Master Craftsmen News

The above represents a full list of all titles currently published or scheduled to be published. All are available direct from the Publishers or through bookshops, newsagents and specialist retailers. To place an order, or to obtain a complete catalogue, contact:

**GMC PUBLICATIONS**
**Castle Place, 166 High Street, Lewes, East Sussex BN7 1XU United Kingdom**
**Tel: 01273 488005  Fax: 01273 402866  E-mail: pubs@thegmcgroup.com**

Orders by credit card are accepted